Lifestyles of The RICH and FAMOUS™

by Robin Leach

with

JUDITH RICH

A Dolphin Book

DOUBLEDAY & COMPANY, INC.

Garden City, New York

1986

Preceding Pages: Carleton Hotel in Cannes (p. 1); Robert Stigwood's yacht in Monaco (pp. 2-3); classic cars from Tom Barrett's collection (inset, p.2); stretch run at Kentucky Derby (inset, p.3); Sultan of Brunei's banquet hall (p. 4)

Produced by Jill Barber

Book design and production by
Kathleen Westray and Ed Sturmer

Library of Congress Cataloging-in-Publication Data

Leach, Robin.
  Lifestyles of the rich and famous.

  "A Dolphin book."
    1. Biography—20th century—Portraits.   2. Upper
classes—Iconography.   3. Lifestyles of the rich and
famous (Television program)—Pictorial works.   I. Rich,
Judith.   II. Lifestyles of the rich and famous (Television program)—Pictorial works.   I. Rich, Judith.
II. Lifestyles of the rich and famous (Television
program)   III. Title.
CT120.L46   1986   920'.009'04   85-25359
ISBN 0-385-23411-2
        0-385-23119-9 (pbk.)

Printed in the United States of America
First Edition

ACKNOWLEDGMENTS

Thanks to: Al Masini, the creative genius and president of TeleRep, Inc., the company that launched the hit weekly series; Phil Flanagan and Mary Jane Hastings and all their staff at Television Program Enterprises, Inc., the team that makes each show possible; Jill Barber, for her determination as producer of this book; Doubleday editor Paul Bresnick, for his guidance and supervision in realizing and bringing to fruition his idea of taking the rich scenes and stories from "Lifestyles" and creatively converting all into a book; Kathleen Westray and Ed Sturmer, for designing the pages in a memorable and accurate reproduction of our weekly TV series; "Lifestyles" photo editor Kas Schlots-Wilson, for tracking down the photos for the myriad of subjects dealt with here. Special thanks to "Lifestyles" writers Jeff Samuels and Leon Freilich and all the staff, especially Elaine Griffin, Laura Gherardi, Greg Bernarducci, and intern Aimee Rentmeester, whose patience, diligence, and good humor made it all possible.

CONTENTS

Portofino

INTRODUCTION

Every week on "Lifestyles of the Rich and Famous" we fulfill the promise we make to our viewers to bring the best of the good life to television.

Since our debut in August 1983, our worldwide camera crews have captured the most fascinating at-home interviews with celebrities, charmed secrets out of multimillionaires, and shot gorgeous interiors of the world's most lavish and opulent homes.

We've become bigger and better with each show, thanks to you. Our mailbag brims over every morning with your questions and requests. In preparing this stunning book, we've set out to give you a permanent record of the very best of "Lifestyles" as a way of answering many of those questions:

"Whose magnificent palace is that?"

"Where's the most elaborate, most expensive penthouse?"

"Whose is the most lavish, most gadget-filled yacht of them all?"

"How does the world's richest man make his money?"

"What's the most exclusive, most remote hideaway in the world?"

"When does influence flow from affluence? And the other way around?"

"What's the price tag on the poshest cruise or jet trip of them all?"

"What's the ultimate shopping spree of the rich and famous?"

Robin Leach with Morgan Fairchild (above) and with Lorenzo Lamas

You'll find the answers in these glittering pages.

It's a lot of fun to track down the astonishing stories that appear on "Lifestyles"—but also a lot of hard work and it takes a loyal and dedicated staff. Producers, directors, writers, production assistants, editors, sound engineers, and cameramen make it all possible. So I'd like to take this opportunity to thank them all. And I'd like to thank all of you as well, for making "Lifestyles of the Rich and Famous" such a successful show week after week. We never forget you because if we didn't put you—the viewer—first and bring you what you want, the TV screen would soon lose the excitement of the twenty-four-karat corridors of success.

We like to think we've pioneered a new form in television. Before we came along, the rewards of hard work and good fortune were seen and appreciated by only a precious few. Now we've brought them out—gloriously—into the open and everyone can share a taste of what this richly endowed planet has to offer and what dreams money can buy. We look forward to bringing you even more magnificent scenes from this infinite treasure trove of success as "Lifestyles" continues.

It's been, and will always remain, a team effort. So when I say each week, "Thank you for joining us," you know it comes from all of us at "Lifestyles."

And remember—you too can be rich and famous and live life to the hilt, fulfilling your champagne wishes and caviar dreams.

Rob Leach!

ROBIN LEACH, the globe-trotting host and producer of "Lifestyles of the Rich and Famous," travels well over a quarter of a million miles a year to nail down the celebrities and mega-millionaires, the sumptuous mansions and exotic hideaways that brighten the hit television series every week.

Born in Harrow, an English town twenty miles from London, Leach embarked on his journalistic career as a reporter for the Harrow *Observer* twenty-eight years ago. Just three years later, he moved up to Fleet Street and the prestigious *Daily Mail.* He moved again in 1963, this time to the United States. From his home base of New York, Leach has been a successful freelance show business reporter ever since, with

With Joan Collins (above), Jennifer O'Neill (below), and Brooke Shields (right)

major articles appearing in magazines like *People, US,* and *Ladies' Home Journal.* Leach has also been a successful publisher. From 1968 to 1971 he published three highly regarded music business publications—*Go* magazine, *R 'n' B World,* and *Stereo Review.* He also wrote two year-in-review books about pop music.

For a full decade, Leach was the world's most widely read celebrity columnist. His weekly show business reports appeared in periodicals ranging from *TV Week* in Australia to *The Star* in America and earned him a loyal readership of 200 million people. He began his career on television with regular appearances on "A.M. Los Angeles" and "Good Morning, New York" and then joined Ted Turner's Cable News Network for two years. From there, he went on to "Entertainment Tonight," where he served as a roving reporter for the top-rated nightly TV series for three years.

Then Leach left to launch his own series, "Lifestyles of the Rich and Famous." It proved an immediate smash, debuting in August 1983 as a two-hour special and racking up a rating of number one "off-network." He also began producing the weekly Steve Allen series "The Start of Something Big," along with several TV specials every year. His latest project is launching the series "Runaway with the Rich and Famous."

Robin Leach is single and lives in a lakefront home in Connecticut—just a gemstone's throw from the rich and famous.

JUDITH RICH is a journalist and television producer who has worked for publications, television news documentaries, and talk and magazine shows in England, the U.S., and her native Australia. She was executive in charge of public relations for the ABC-TV network's San Francisco station and runs her own promotion company.

RUNAWAYS

Brooke Shields in Africa

When I accompanied Brooke Shields, the world's most-photographed superstar, on an African wildlife safari for "Lifestyles," it was the fulfillment of her dream to see the animals she loves in all their natural splendor. Our safari covered two thousand miles in five grueling days, crossing the equator twice as it swung up into the forests of Mount Kenya and down to the endless plains of the Masai Mara.

Our starting point was a magical place called Giraffe Manor, just outside Nairobi, where she awakened in the morning to find gentle giraffes staring in the window. The world's best-known cover girl was soon to encounter the most feared warriors of the African continent, the Masai, who greeted her with a ritualistic drink of fresh cow's blood in their village on the floor of the great Rift Valley.

Then out of the skies above the Serengeti Plain came an envoy of private planes sent by one of the world's richest men, Adnan Khashoggi, with an invitation for us to his sprawling 15,000-acre Kenyan ranch. Brooke was taken on a thrilling jeep ride into his private preserve of twenty-seven wild lions. She watched in horror and fascination as the hungry lions leaped upon the flatbed truck to devour hunks of freshly slaughtered meat.

The next day we flew over the largest migration of animals in the world—20 million hooves thundered across the veldt in search of new pastures, just as they have done for millions of years. We landed at one of the most luxurious hotels in the world for lunch. Founded by William Holden, the late preservationist actor, in 1959, the immaculately pruned, one-thousand-acre Mount Kenya Safari Club has been a home away from home for celebrity travelers like Sir Winston Churchill, Clark Gable, John Wayne, and Bob Hope.

In the awesome calm of the Masai Mara, we spent the night in tents at an unusual canvas hotel, Governor's Camp. Another breathtaking experience came at Treetops, the most unique hotel in the world, built in the heart of the bush as an observation platform in the branches of a chestnut tree, overlooking a watering hole. We sipped champagne while watching the wild beasts come in. For Brooke, who has worked with animals at San Diego Zoo, our African safari was a privileged view of untamed nature. She told me: "Coming out here and just seeing vast areas of land with animals thundering by, it's very relaxing. It makes me feel very, very free. It's like a reward."

Morgan Fairchild in Venice

Venice, one of the most unusual and dazzling cities in the world, has cast its spell of enchantment on world travelers for centuries. The towers and domes of the glistening city on the lagoon, known as "The Serene One," are much the same today as when Marco Polo returned home in triumph from China. For hundreds of years, Venice served as "The Gateway to the Orient." Now the waterways, arched by charming bridges, are still filled with bustling boats and gliding gondolas.

Lovely actress Morgan Fairchild stepped off the Orient Express into a water taxi for an unforgettable ride through the ancient canals to the legendary Cipriani Hotel near San Marco Square. "This city is to be revered for how long it has withstood time and especially the elements, being built the way it is on little islands," says Morgan. "The really beautiful thing about a city like this is that you realize the insignificance of any one life in terms of world history."

French Riviera

For centuries the French Riviera has upheld a grand, classic tradition as Europe's most fashionable playground. With its sumptuous stucco palaces, regal hotels, majestic promenades, picturesque townships, and ports crowded with the world's largest yachts, the Côte d'Azur draws the chic international set—Roger Moore, Cher, Jeanne Moreau, Charles Aznavour, Harold Robbins, and billionaire Adnan Khashoggi.

Like a string of pearls, the famous resort towns glow with a luminous, seductive charm—Cannes, St.-Tropez, Nice, Juan-les-Pins, Antibes, and the hillside getaways of St.-Paul-de-Vence and Villefranche. Old-world grace blends with today's casual chic, as sun worshippers garnish topless beaches, party all night at opulent clubs, or retreat to rented villas and farmhouses in the vineyards and olive groves, while the gentle mistral breezes blow in from the Mediterranean.

Aspen

. . . .

Aspen, Colorado, is the winter watering hole of the stars, where big-name visitors are eclipsed only by the awesome beauty of the terrain. John Denver called it "Rocky Mountain High" and makes it his full-time residence. Sheiks, politicians, and the rich and famous keep lavish second homes here. Celebrities hooked on Aspen include Diana Ross, Jill St. John, Jack Nicholson —seen here riding the ski lift—and Barbi Benton— sporting her ski bunny outfit here with millionaire husband George Gradow.

With an elevation of 11,800 feet, Aspen offers some of the best skiing in the world. It's a stunning setting, where the rich and famous trade their Gucci shoes for cowboy boots and their Rolls-Royces for jeeps and Blazers. Mealtimes find hungry skiers dining on oysters Rockefeller and caviar at Ruthie's Polo Club and when it comes to shopping, this charming old mining town rivals Fifth Avenue for chic.

Nepal and Kashmir, India

On the rooftop of the world, high in the Himalayas, is
the exotic kingdom of Nepal, with its remote mountain
monastaries and centuries' old temples of solid gold
and erotic stone carvings, and where the Yeti, the elu-
sive abominable snowman, frolics in the rarified air.
Until the late sixties, few tourists could visit this for-
bidden Shangri-la, nestled amid the peaks of Mount
Everest, the highest mountain in the world, and An-
napurna. Stars Pam Dawber and Persis Khambatta are
among modern-day pilgrims who've made this timeless
journey.

In the medieval back streets of Kathmandu, capital
of Nepal, they came upon the temple of the Kumari,

named for a girl-child worshipped as a virgin goddess.
Once she reaches puberty, the Kumari's likely fate is a
life of prostitution because locals believe a man who
marries a Kumari will die young. On the Street of
Happy Mouths, with one thousand dentists, they discovered the legendary toothache tree, with powers of
healing that give instant relief from pain—and following tradition, they drove a nail into its trunk as preven-
tive medicine.

Then it was a two-and-a-half-hour elephant ride

through the southern lowlands to the curious treehouse hotel of Tiger Tops, where the guest list has included Robert Redford, Goldie Hawn, Kurt Russell and "Dynasty" star Pamela Bellwood, who was married here in 1985 to British photographer Nik Wheeler. Tiger Tops, in the heart of Chitwan National Park, is the last refuge of the endangered Bengal tiger.

The Vale of Kashmir, in a high Himalayan valley in northwest India, has been famed for its natural beauty since the days of the Moghul Emperors and it was here that one built the fragrant lakeside Gardens of Shalimar. In the unhurried waterborn society of lotus-eaters, Persis, and Pam took a *shikara,* or water taxi, to tour the mirrored splendors of Lake Dal. When the British ruled India, they built houseboats on the water to circumvent the Maharaja's ban against their owning land—and the decorative houseboats are still the preferred accommodation for residents and visitors alike.

Lana Turner in Egypt

. . . .

Legendary screen actress Lana Turner has traveled the world during her forty-year career, but no place on earth has exerted such an extraordinary power on her as Egypt—even before she ever went there. "I was always being drawn more and more to it," said Lana, who at age sixty-three had her dream fulfilled when we took a regal trip back in time to the Valley of the Kings—burial ground for the rulers of Egypt. "I believe in reincarnation and I know I have been here before. How many thousands of years ago, I'm not quite sure, but I keep feeling fulfillment coming in."

Here in the shadows of the Giza Pyramids, dating back to 2700 B.C., guarded by the enigmatic Sphinx, a great mystery stirs the soul. On her first-ever visit, we rode camels across the shifting sands to the majestic pyramids for a privileged visit to the 3,200-year-old tomb of the boy king Tutankhamen, which lay undiscovered till 1922. "Why, I don't know, but there's a very, very deep spiritual and psychological reason for me to be here at this very moment," whispered Lana.

Cruising aboard the *Nile Pharaoh,* she lunched with Mrs. Anwar Sadat, widow of the assassinated Egyptian president. In

Cairo, she stayed in an 1869 palace, now a Sheraton hotel, built by Khedive Ismail to celebrate the opening of the Suez Canal and to entice Empress Eugénie of France to visit him. Legend has it that the beautiful Empress spent just one night there.

Everywhere Lana went in Cairo's famous bazaars, the locals gave her a royal welcome. She will never forget how she felt so strangely at home in Egypt.

Valerie Perrine in Champagne Country

It's the sparkling companion to any celebration . . . the favorite drink of the rich and famous—champagne. Actress Valerie Perrine's journey to trace her French ancestry took her to the Champagne region, where she visited Château de Saran, the 1820 castle of the Moët & Chandon family, whose vineyards have produced some of the world's finest champagne. Early in this century a special blend of champagne was created for the private consumption of the Moët & Chandon family. It was called Dom Pérignon, after the French monk who first came up with a method of making champagne from wines that came from these hillsides.

Count Ghislain de Vogue swept Valerie up in his hot air balloon for a bird's-eye view of the company's 1,250 acres of vineyards. Beneath this spectacular estate are stored 75 million bottles of champagne in eighteen miles of cellars. Nearby are the famous champagne houses of Bollinger, Mumm, and Roederer.

Palm Springs

The desert resort of Palm Springs is home to countless celebrities and even has streets and drives named after some of its most famous residents—like Frank Sinatra, Bob Hope, and Gerald Ford. It's Hollywood's favorite playpen, a natural sun-trap one hundred miles away, where it's always summer. While Palm Springs has only thirty-five thousand residents, over one hundred thousand visitors regularly pour in on a winter weekend. The town's forty golf courses make it the golf capital of the world and there are plenty of places to cool off when the mercury hits the hundred mark. More than seven thousand swimming pools dot the desert paradise.

Las Hadas

One of the world's most exotic tropical playgrounds, Las Hadas, rises like a dream vision on Mexico's magnificent Pacific coast. The white Moorish spires and domes of this spectacular village emerge from the lush jungles of the Santiago Peninsula. Marble-lined cobblestone paths wind upward from the pristine beaches of Manzanillo Bay.

At the center of this Gold Coast jewel is the Hotel Las Hadas, where islands and waterfalls fringe the lagoon-sized pool and guests who stay in the deluxe suites can frolic in their own private pools, with fresh flowers floating on the surface each day, compliments of room service. Las Hadas gained fame when Dudley Moore and Bo Derek filmed "10" along its beaches. Many wealthy Americans have built multimillion-dollar homes overlooking the ocean and the port is a haven for the yachts of the rich and famous.

St. James's Club, Antigua

Antigua is an exotic paradise in the British West Indies —the only Caribbean island with 365 sandy beaches, one for every day of the year. The ultimate tropical playpen for the rich and famous is the St. James's Club, an exclusive one-hundred-acre resort in Antigua —strictly members only.

Wealthy British entrepreneur Peter de Savory spent over $20 million renovating and creating this hideaway haven for jet-set hedonists. De Savory's St. James's Club in London opened in 1981, has five thousand members, and is so popular with stars and socialites that he decided to take his luxury concept down south and plans more in Los Angeles, New York, and Europe next year.

For club members, including Joan Collins, actor Michael York, Sir John Mills, Liza Minnelli, and Ann-Margret, the unspoiled Antigua location is a perfect paparazzi-free hideaway, well worth the steep price of admission. A vacation here can range from the least expensive, $600 a night for a double room, to $1,000 plus per night for a seaside villa.

Portofino—
with Jacklyn Zeman

· · · · · · · · · · · · · · · ·

Portofino is a tiny Italian Riviera seaport, with the world's most fabulous yachts packed into its sheltering harbor. It's both a wealthy resort and a typically small coastal town, where romantic sun-drenched afternoons are spent sipping drinks on the waterfront piazza. This was a perfect getaway for one of daytime television's busiest stars, Jacklyn Zeman, who came to work on her beauty and fitness book. "I had heard that Portofino is one of the most beautiful places in the world and truly it is," she says. "The thing that impressed me most about it was pulling in on a boat, seeing the flowers, the colors."

It was Jacklyn's first vacation in seven years and a dream come true for the "General Hospital" TV star when she cruised the azure Mediterranean Sea on a yacht: "I've always loved the water. The idea of getting to be on a boat and not having to put any makeup on for a month was very appealing to me."

Rio de Janeiro

Jet-setters from all over the world flock to this South American city for its breathtaking views and the zest of its vibrant Brazilian natives. Every year the entire city erupts with the sensual Carnival and everyone lets down their hair in the world's wildest nonstop costume party. For those who want their beach experience to vibrate with the sound of the gentle samba, Rio's sweeping sands of Copacabana and Ipanema fill the bill. Rio is the city that created the tantalizing *tonga,* a string bikini so tiny it's called "El Band-Aid." Under the protective eye of Sugar Loaf Mountain, Rio's panoramic vistas and bay are so dramatically beautiful they outshine any in the world.

Ipanema (above) and Copacabana (opposite)

Overleaf: Houseboats on Lake Dal, Kashmir

Pam Dawber in India

Persis Khambatta in India

U.S. Virgin Islands

In the Caribbean lie the U.S. Virgin Islands, temples of temptation beckoning the wealthy world travelers. Once a Danish colony, trade center, and rendezvous of pirates, St. Thomas is second in size to St. Croix, and its port is filled with luxury yachts—turning it into a millionaire's parking lot. The narrow streets of this free port are fast becoming the Rodeo Drive of the Caribbean, lined with the expensive shops of Yves Saint Laurent, Guy Laroche, Cartier, and Cardow, which boasts the largest jewelry selection in the world. As the strains of disco calypso float on the gentle trade winds, the hills of St. Thomas come alive with the sound of . . . money! Names like Dupont, Gucci, and Countess Paolozzi have hideaway homes on the island and property prices have skyrocketed. The crystal waters of Magen's Bay, one of the most beautiful beaches in the world, coax the lucky lotus-eaters to abandon themselves.

On the island of St. John privileged vacationers languish on the exclusive beaches of Caneel Bay, private reserve of one of the world's richest men, Laurance Rockefeller. High-powered luminaries, including Henry Kissinger and the Aga Khan, stayed at this former eighteenth-century plantation, with 168 guest rooms in 170 tropically landscaped acres, only steps away from seven golden beaches. Celebrities who come to frolic on this secluded peninsula include Mel Brooks, Anne Bancroft, Carol Burnett, Jill Clayburgh, Frank Langella, Rita Moreno, and Alan Alda, who filmed parts of *The Four Seasons* here. Privacy is assured and the only way in is by water—on a private yacht or ferry.

RAGS TO RICHES

Rick James

James Johnson left the ghettos of Buffalo, New York, to become "Super Freak" superstar Rick James and ride a wave of success to the top of the record charts, selling 15 million copies of one album alone. But the road to stardom led Rick right back to where it all began. When his career really started to take off in 1978, Rick bought a home in the country outside Buffalo, with a recording studio, indoor pool, Jacuzzi, tennis court, and horses.

"It's a sanctuary for me and it really gives me a good balance on life," says Rick. "It's a real nice place to be, to know that your roots are right next to you and whenever you need them for strength, you go there."

Rick sometimes still visits the small old two-bedroom house deep in the ghetto, where he grew up in a family of four boys and four girls. His mother Betty supported the family by running numbers and working in hospitals. She has always been an inspiration and today she lives in Rick's home with him. "I'm very proud of my mother," he says. "She raised eight kids and I'm not ashamed to say what my mother did. She ran numbers to keep us all eating."

Rick inherited that determination. "I had always felt that I was a star. To me I was a star, although I was broke and could not afford to eat." When he struck gold, Rick fulfilled his dream, blowing millions on high living. But the dream turned into a nightmare in 1979, when drug abuse put him in the hospital and he discovered he was a million dollars in debt because of embezzled money. Broke and sick, he made a decision to turn his life around.

He wrote new songs and started regaining his health. He put out his biggest album, *Street Songs,* which sold 15 million records. Rick threw himself right back into the high-voltage world of rock and roll and today he's a powerhouse in the industry, not only handling his own career but producing and managing a family of other bands.

Rocky Aoki

Rocky Aoki was once so poor he had nowhere to sleep but in the men's room of his first restaurant. He also cheated death seven times and today is one of life's richest winners. He runs an international restaurant chain grossing $75 million annually and has made so much money that he once smiled off a $30-million business loss.

Rocky's road to riches started with the Benihana Restaurant concept, which combines the deceptively simple ingredients of showmanship and the American love of a short-order grill. Add to that the Benihana frozen oriental food line, which does around $3 million in business a month and is well on its way to making Rocky another $100-million company.

Flying between his $20-million cattle ranch in Japan, his seventy restaurants, and his headquarters in New York and Miami, Rocky covers a quarter of a million miles a year.

Twenty years ago, when Rocky arrived here from Japan, he had only $200 in his pocket and spoke no English. He worked seventeen hours a day selling ice cream on the streets of Harlem—the first business he owned. He opened his first Benihana in 1964, named after his father's tiny coffee shop in Japan. It means "red flower."

At one point in his rags-to-riches life, Rocky owned five houses, an airplane, and forty cars, including eighteen Rolls-Royces, Ferraris, Bentleys, and Maseratis. His unusual 1972 stretch limousine is the first of its kind ever ordered from Mercedes.

His incredible inner drives have forged a business and a fortune which give him the excuse and the means to live an outrageously daring lifestyle. In 1974 he inaugurated the Benihana Grand Prix—a world-class offshore power boat race which he won a few times. But in 1979 a boat disintegrated under him in San Francisco Bay and he was pronounced dead on arrival. He broke two legs, lost his spleen and gall bladder. Open-heart surgery and the insertion of a Dacron aorta saved his life. But barely two years later he was back at it and rebroke both legs in another race. "I think I'm a born challenger," says Rocky, who was also a former Japanese Olympic wrestler.

Mickey Gilley

. . . .

After seventeen number one records and the success of the John
Travolta–Debra Winger film based on his honky-tonk club, Mickey Gilley
is finally able to afford a high-flying lifestyle—with his own personalized
jet—to match his high-flying career.

Success didn't come easy for high school dropout Mickey Gilley, a poor
boy from Louisiana who, like John Travolta in *Urban Cowboy,* paid the
bills working construction. Mickey's recording career had more ups and
downs than the mechanical bull in his club. Overshadowed by the success
of his cousin Jerry Lee Lewis, Mickey waited until 1974 for a hit. Those
fifteen years were filled with gigs at small honky-tonks in and around
Houston. A chance meeting one day with the owner of a Houston club led
to the launch of Gilley's.

The club holds 3,500 cowboys and sprawls over three acres, complete
with Gilley's own indoor rodeo. Gilley's empire also includes a Houston
recording studio and a staff of thirty to manage his $4 million worth of
concert dates and merchandising deals every year.

But this man who earns well over $6 million a year continued to live
very simply for nineteen years in a modest suburban home he bought for
$14,000 with his wife Vivian and their son. Only recently did they build a
new $2-million dream house, complete with a music room and full record-
ing studio, tennis court, swimming pool, and a lake stocked with fish.

Diahann Carroll

The daughter of a Harlem subway conductor, she grew up dreaming of a show business career. Diahann Carroll's dream came true when she became the first black actress to star in a prime-time television sitcom in 1968. In "Julia," her portrayal of a young beautiful widowed mom sparked controversy because she was too nice. Today Diahann has turned vixen, playing the villainous Dominique Devereaux on the hit series "Dynasty," a role that has put her on top of the world again in a roller-coaster career spanning three decades.

Diahann always set her sights high, even as a child of a working-class family. But she spent many lean years as a singer, traveling alone around the country, performing at nightclubs and hotels. "I don't ever want to be that vulnerable," she says. "I don't know how I did it. I was obviously so determined and I needed it so much that nothing else mattered."

That single-mindedness paid off. Diahann was living high, with her Bentley auto, a big mansion and staff, indulging her penchant for fine clothing and wine. Today she has scaled down her extravagance, enjoying a bicoastal lifestyle between a smaller home, filled with valuable art, in the palm trees and one in New York, where she feels more comfortable. With two marriages behind her, she has found love with longtime companion singer Vic Damone. Her television comeback has fired up the "Dynasty" ratings and life is as exciting as ever.

Loretta Lynn

In the Kentucky coal mining community of Butcher Hollow, a young girl's sweet voice would drift across the valley as she serenaded her younger brothers and sisters on the porch of the family shack. No one dreamed it was the start of a country singing legend known simply as "The Coal Miner's Daughter." Today Loretta Lynn calls a beautiful 3,500-acre ranch outside Nashville home. But an abandoned shack on the grounds is a constant reminder of her humble beginnings. "When I'm down there I think of what I did have and what did drive me to make sure that my kids didn't have to live like that."

Loretta's backwoods-to-bright-lights struggle with Mooney Lynn, the husband who believed in her, paid off and Loretta's music was a resounding hit. "You can always pull yourself out," says Loretta. "Just keep right on working. I tell you, it's hard work, but you can make anything of yourself."

Loretta and Mooney, whom she married at just fourteen years old, had four children, and only $100 in savings, which they gambled to produce her first single, "Honky-Tonk Girl." Loretta says, "Even though we did have nothing when we were young, we were rich when it came to love." "The Coal Miner's Daughter" is today "The Queen of Country Music," but she never forgets her meager beginnings, with barely enough to feed the family. She still keeps a year's supply of food in her pantry "because you never know when we may need that."

SUPERSTARS

John Forsythe

As the suave, debonair patriarch of the Carrington dynasty, John Forsythe leads a life of excess in a sumptuous mansion. But Forsythe is fulfilling his own fantasy of success with the dream home he built and an active outdoor lifestyle. He doesn't take his image as America's sixty-five-year-old sex symbol too seriously. His marriage to former actress Julie Warren has lasted thirty-nine years and they've raised two children, plus a son by Forsythe's previous marriage.

The new handcrafted white sandstone home looks out on eucalyptus and sycamore trees—a more rustic setting than the New England-style home they've occupied in Bel Air. It's a three-story English-style manor, perfectly fitting for the English antique furniture Forsythe and his interior decorator wife have collected on vacations in Britain. They also have an art collection of impressionist and modern paintings. The showpiece living room–den is thirty-five by thirty-five feet, with a marble fireplace, oaken bar, and a stained-glass window.

Forsythe has always been sports oriented. He started as a baseball play-by-play announcer before becoming the actor who was best known for his 1957–62 hit series "Bachelor Father." With a solar-heated swimming pool, sauna, gym, and tennis court, Forsythe can pursue the physical activities he enjoys. Exercise became a necessity after his quadruple bypass surgery in 1979. He also likes to relax from his demanding "Dynasty" schedule by heading out into the Pacific on his thirty-foot sailboat.

But his first love is horse racing. He owns sixteen horses; one of his mares, Targa, won six races and well over a quarter of a million dollars before retiring, and is worth a fortune today. "Horses are more than a hobby; they've become a business for me," says Forsythe. "To breed horses and see the whole process of training that leads up to the race is like seeing your children in the Olympics." What more would he want to complete his happily rounded lifestyle? "I would gladly give up an Academy Award to win the Kentucky Derby."

Burt Reynolds

Burt Reynolds's macho image and sex appeal made him a hot box-office property and earned him $5 million a picture. As one of Hollywood's most notorious Romeos, Burt left a long line of Hollywood ladies brokenhearted because he refused to take the marital plunge. Since his three-year marriage to British "Laugh In" star Judy Carne ended in 1966, bachelor Burt's love life has been as hot as his daring debut in *Playgirl* magazine as the first male nude centerfold.

His romances with Dinah Shore, nineteen years his senior, and Oscar-winner Sally Field matured him, but couldn't still his restless search for love. His longtime love, Loni Anderson, shared his two-story Spanish-style home, where Western paintings decorate the walls and he can roll out of bed into the swimming pool or gym. But Burt's mornings often start far away from the Hollywood spotlight—on his secluded 170-acre ranch in Jupiter, Florida, where he rides horses at dawn. Over the years, he's had his black-and-gold chopper standing by to fly in his current love and his own VIP box at his nearby Burt Reynolds Dinner Theatre. The ranch, built in the 1920s by gangster Al Capone as a hideout, is Burt's getaway, where he can get fit and enjoy the restorative powers of nature.

With Loni Anderson

Raquel Welch

Raquel Welch revealed the secrets of her fabulous figure and sensuality in a book titled *Raquel,* along with a video shot against the stunning backdrop of the Caribbean island of Mustique, where she has spent many vacations.

"Most people think of me as this sort of big strapping kind of voluptuary and actually people who know me in person know I am kind of a tiny girl," she says. "I am a size-six dress and I am not really what you call a female jock. I have always flunked out of aerobics and jogging and weightlifting and everything that I have tried to stay in shape with over the years. So when I found something I could do, I figured anyone—everyone—could do it."

Raquel, age forty-five, lives in a New York apartment overlooking Central Park with her European husband Andre Weinfeld, who shot the photographs for her book and produced and directed the video. But Raquel is a Southern California girl who was a cheerleader at La Jolla High School and misses the more relaxing West Coast lifestyle.

She has this to say to women on many issues: "I want them to get a sense, if they can hear my voice, a feeling of optimism, enthusiasm . . . like, you can do it! You don't have to do it great and you don't have to be perfect . . . just do it. This or anything else you want to do in life—just be nice to yourself. Don't be ruthless, don't beat yourself up, don't judge yourself. Just live."

Robert Wagner

In the style of his multimillionaire globe-trotting character in television's "Hart to Hart," Robert Wagner is at home in the international playgrounds of the world. He owns a home in Gstaad, Switzerland, where he spends winters skiing. Since the tragic death of his wife Natalie Wood in 1981, Wagner has devoted himself to his three teenage daughters: Courtney, Natasha, and Katherine. He gave up his Beverly Hills home for a secluded San Fernando Valley ranch. A horse owner since childhood, Wagner keeps Arabian stallions in stables on his ranch. He shares a love of polo with former costar Stephanie Powers, whose close friendship helped him through the trauma of his loss.

Wagner is romantically linked with actress Jill St. John, who shares his love of skiing and the mountains at her Aspen home and on visits to Gstaad. "I enjoy the mountains a lot," says Wagner. "I enjoy that life over there. You know when actors act, they work very hard and when they play, they play."

Robert Wagner—father and superstar—makes the most of the rarefied air at the top of the mountain.

Victoria Principal

As the sweet and sexy Pamela Ewing, "Dallas" star Victoria Principal collects an estimated $50,000 paycheck per episode. But Victoria is a sharp business executive who's capitalizing on her talents from hair product promotions and her best-selling series of health and beauty books. Her burgeoning financial interests include film producing and real estate holdings, including her own homes in Beverly Hills and Palm Springs and a residence she built for her parents in Atlanta.

Victoria was an Air Force brat whose family never stayed in one place for very long and she grew up with a craving to feel part of a community. Today she has put down roots and is a highly respected member of the Beverly Hills community. Her Benedict Canyon home reflects her love of nature in earth tones that somehow recall the earthiness of the summers she spent as a child at her grandmother's farm in Georgia —the only place she felt any sense of belonging.

The ultimate ingredient in Victoria's principles for a happy life was marriage to Beverly Hills plastic surgeon Dr. Harry Glassman. "I feel as though I have for the first time in my life, the last few years, found a balance, a very healthy, complete balance, where the work is not the only thing in my life and my personal relationships and my family and vacations and the work all have their place and their priorities, but things aren't out of perspective," Victoria says.

Julio Iglesias

The seductive sounds of Julio Iglesias have made him the most popular singer in the world today, with best-selling albums in over sixty countries. He's sold 300 gold records, 100 platinum records, and is the only recording artist ever to sell more than 100 million albums in six languages.

The undisputed Don Juan of pop leads a globe-trotting lifestyle, with homes in Madrid, Majorca, Argentina, and Tahiti. He's also at home in Bel Air, where the shade of his enormous blue pool is reflected indoors in his master bedroom suite, and on private Indian Creek Island, where his $6-million mansion looks across to Miami and is designed with lounging areas of luxurious sofas where Julio can fall asleep anytime in any room. Julio leads a bachelor existence, always surrounded by adoring women. He has three children from his first and only marriage, which ended in 1979. He has two Rolls-Royces and an $87,000 custom-made Clenet, but prefers to tool around Florida in a Volkswagen Rabbit. In Miami he has a yacht he never gets to use and a helicopter he's afraid to fly in.

The son of a prominent physician in Madrid, Julio's soccer career and law studies came to a shattering halt when a crippling auto accident left him hospitalized for a year. One fateful day a nurse gave him a guitar and Julio took his first determined steps toward a mercurial music career.

Today his life is mostly on the road, particularly since an unprecedented multimillion-dollar marketing deal with Coca-Cola took him on a nonstop forty-six country tour. The young man who nearly spent his life confined to a wheelchair has conquered the hearts of a worldwide audience with his tantalizing love songs.

Performing with the Beach Boys (above)

Linda Evans

As the exquisite cut-glass Krystle Carrington in "Dynasty," Linda Evans has touched a familiar nerve in women viewers and won the hearts of millions. "When I read the script I felt Krystle was so much like me," she says. "A woman living for a man and feeling that no matter what happens, love will take care of everything." Linda learned otherwise from her own marriages to two men who she says dominated her—actor John Derek and wealthy realtor Stan Herman—which both ended in divorce.

Today Linda is fulfilling the prophecy of a card reader who once told her she'd enjoy her greatest happiness and success in her mature years. She's found inner contentment in her charming Beverly Hills home, decorated in country French with oriental overtones. Filled with greenery, the house has rich wood downstairs and feminine pastels upstairs. After a day on the "Dynasty" set, she can relax with a massage and potter in her garden, where there's a pool and a Japanese pond. She enjoys cooking for friends and maintains her stunning form in a gym off the kitchen. "To me beauty is something inside," says the forty-two-year-old actress. "You can say someone looks pretty or handsome, but to me that's not the most important element. If we'd start realizing that we're just wonderful, if we love ourselves, then more people will look at us and see beauty."

Linda has come a long way since actor John Forsythe gave her that first big break at the age of fifteen, casting her in his hit series "Bachelor Father." Today she plays the wife of the patriarch of the Carrington clan. She's found confidence in her personal life after making it on her own. "I've always felt I was late in growing up and I've finally learned you can be in love without giving your whole life to the relationship."

Tom Jones

. . . .

Fame and fortune have carried
superstar Tom Jones thousands of
miles from the tiny Welsh mining
village of Pontypridd, where as a
lad he worked in a paper mill by
day and sang in his local pub by
night. Since his first smash, "It's
Not Unusual," twenty years ago,
he's collected more than fifty gold
and platinum records.

Jones traded a tiny coal miner's
house for a spectacular home in Bel
Air, California. "I had bought this
beautiful brick Tudor house in England and I loved it," says Jones.
"So when I moved to America I
didn't want to leave the house
there, so I thought if I could dupli-
cate it in some way . . . and this
house is identical." Jones shipped
his furniture, including an English
bar, across the Atlantic to make
him feel at home. His most mean-
ingful piece is the phone booth
from his Welsh village that he once
used to call a local sweetheart.

Jones is married to that same
sweetheart, Linda. He regularly
plays squash with his son, who has
made the sexy superstar a grandfather. While Linda prefers to stay in
the background, Jones is out front
—and on the road—nine months of
the year. His famous sexy gyrations
incite hundreds of his female fans
at every show to toss their room
keys, wrapped in lacy panties, at
his dancing feet. At Caesars Palace
in Las Vegas alone, five thousand
keys have been collected from the
stage.

With grandson at home

Jacqueline Bisset
. . . .

British actress Jacqueline Bisset is
one of Hollywood's most sought-af-
ter stars. Since her movie debut in
1965, she's starred in more than
thirty films that have taken her to
the world's most exotic locations.
Her onscreen romances have
matched her with leading men, including Nick Nolte, Paul Newman,
Ryan O'Neal, and Albert Finney.
The late French director Francois
Truffaut wooed her while shaping
her radiant performance in *Day for
Night.*

   Green-eyed beauty Jackie shares
her quaint white stone house off
Beverly Hills' Benedict Canyon with
dashing Russian ballet dancer Alex-
ander Godunov, the man in her life
for five years. For her fortieth
birthday, when Jackie was in Hun-
gary filming *Anna Karenina,* Godunov sent champagne and a trio of
violinists to her hotel in Budapest.
Jackie and her handsome lover lead
a jet-set life on location or on tour
around the world—but they always
find a way to put romance into
their busy schedule.

Roger Moore

. . . .

As the supersuave secret agent 007, Roger Moore survives death plots, takes his vodka martinis "shaken, not stirred," and makes love to the world's most exotic women. The son of a London policeman who was fired from his first job for pocketing expense money, Moore now enjoys all the refinements and none of the hazards of a James Bond existence. The urbane and debonair actor earns a reported $4 million for each Bond film and is a sex symbol to women everywhere.

He and his Italian wife Luisa have homes in the French Riviera and Switzerland. In their walled mountaintop village of St.-Paul-de-Vence, an artist colony for decades, they often dine at the renowned Colombe d'Or restaurant, once frequented by some of the century's greatest painters, including Picasso, Braque, Miró, Matisse, Léger, and Dufy. In the Swiss Alpine resort of Gstaad, Moore's greatest pleasure is stepping out of his front door onto the slopes to indulge his passion for skiing.

The unflappable, charismatic Moore style made its mark on the British series "The Saint," which brought him fame in its six-and-a-half-year run. He's slipped smoothly into seven Bond thrillers, taking him to glamorous locations around the world. "The basic formula is similar in all Bonds," he says. "The villain, the heroine, just the same as the fairy story you tell a child every night. They like the same story. The far-out action, adventure, entertainment—that goes in all countries. They want to be taken out of themselves. Escapism."

That winning box-office chemistry has enabled Moore to escape the pressures of a show business career and live in the most enchanting playgrounds in the world.

With wife Luisa and children in Gstaad

David Hasselhoff

David Hasselhoff is living every man's dream. Onscreen, as the star of the "Knight Rider" TV series, he's the idol of millions of teenage girls, getting his thrills with some pretty fancy driving behind the wheel of a speeding James Bond-type car. His meteoric rise to fame has earned him the giant Hollywood movie star playhouse he fantasized about as a boy, with four bedrooms, five bathrooms, a pool, Jacuzzi, tennis court, game room, and an African room filled with pieces he collected on his world travels. He's married to gorgeous actress Catherine Hickland and they share their elegant home with two parrots; one of them sings opera.

At age thirty, David Hasselhoff has it made. But he's astute enough to go even further, translating his "Knight Rider" success into big business with a Rag Ball softball. His image is now on lunch boxes, sleeping bags, T-shirts, posters, and a Halloween costume with a mask of his face. There's even a "Knight Rider" toothpaste dispenser. "It's very important to me, especially right now, to make hay while the sun shines," he says.

With wife Catherine Hickland

Tom Selleck

"Magnum, P.I." star Tom Selleck has found paradise in the tropical Hawaiian island setting of his hit TV series. Since its premiere in 1980, Selleck has catapulted to fame as one of the biggest stars in episodic television, earning $50,000-plus per weekly show. The strapping six-foot-four-inch actor, who once posed for Salem billboard ads, has been compared to such romantic screen heroes as Clark Gable and Burt Reynolds.

But when the actors' strike stalled the production of "Magnum," Selleck was forced to do handyman work—gardening, building fences, and painting—to keep up the rent on his Honolulu house. He eventually bought the beachside community home, worth $500,000, and often has his stepson Kevin from his eleven-year marriage to model-actress Jacquelyn Ray (which ended in 1982) and his parents and siblings in for visits. A gifted athlete who won a four-year basketball scholarship to U.S.C., Selleck is a volleyball fanatic and plays alongside Olympians at Oahu's exclusive Outrigger Canoe Club, competing on their team.

The forty-one-year-old sex symbol, who attracts crowds of adoring women whenever he steps out for a day's shooting, has become "The Pineapple Isle's" biggest attraction. As the soft Pacific breezes rustle through the palm trees on Waikiki's shores, Tom Selleck can truly feel he's living a dream.

Barbara Cartland

Every afternoon Barbara Cartland lies on the sofa at her castle estate with her two poodles beside her and one of her four secretaries seated out of view behind her. In a trance, she dictates an astonishing seven thousand words a day, cranking out twenty-six novels a year. "It's all extraordinary because it comes from my subconscious," she says.

Cartland, age eighty-two and as English as tea and crumpets, is the undisputed "Queen of Romance." She's penned 375 books and sold 400 million copies in more than a dozen languages. "I happen to be the only author who has 150 virgins lying about," she says of her heroines.

Saving chastity and starry-eyed romance from extinction has brought her a 400-acre estate, Camfield Place, forty miles outside London, with an all-pink twelve-bathroom Victorian mansion and a Rolls-Royce. Her lifestyle is eloquent testimony to the winning Cartland formula that doesn't just stop at paperbacks. She has packaged the concept of romance into a million-dollar trademark on her own line of herbal sachets, jigsaw puzzles, sheets, towels, wallpaper, computer games, and vitamins.

Barbara Taylor Bradford

Barbara Taylor Bradford holds millions of readers captive with her stories of passion, sex, and success. Her first novel, *A Woman of Substance,* sold 11 million copies and 35 million people watched the highly rated TV miniseries. But Barbara was so uncertain of her writing talents, when she first went to work on a newspaper in England at age sixteen, that she burned her typed pages in the ladies' room after hours when everyone had gone home.

She's become a permanent fixture on the American best-seller lists, with a second novel, *Voice of the Heart,* and a sequel to the saga of indomitable Emma Harte, *Hold the Dream.* She commands multimillion-dollar advances, which allow her to live a luxurious lifestyle in a lavish penthouse on Manhattan's fashionable Upper East Side. She shares her beige- and peach-toned apartment with husband of twenty-two years Bob Bradford, who produces her miniseries, and Gemmy, a Bichon Frise dog who is her companion during the long hours of writing in her study.

Their home is furnished with natural materials—cedar-lined closets, suede-covered chairs, Italian linen walls. The Hermès leather-lined bookcase in the living room contains antique objects, such as a pair of nineteenth-century white Staffordshire dogs from Barbara's exquisite collection of old porcelains and pottery. In the elegant dining room a Georgian crystal chandelier hangs amid mirrored beams and carved niches display her collections of antique cranberry and blue glass.

With another gold-plated novel, *Act of Will,* under her belt, the future looks bright for Barbara. "To me the excitement is that I can do something that I love—which is writing novels—and get paid a lot of money."

Kenny Rogers

He's one of America's most popular and prolific entertainers and with $250 million worth of record sales and a $20 million-plus RCA recording contract Kenny Rogers is the king of a new breed of country music stars. The once down-home country and western music scene is big business today, and Rogers represents a mega-mogul aristocracy of stars whose cowboy boots are made for walking a multimillion-dollar road of success. He plows most of his income into real estate and at one point had three homes that alone were worth $35 million.

Rogers's numerous hits often have a social message. But his hit song "She Believes in Me" has a special meaning for Rogers and his fourth wife, Marianne, who met him while he was struggling for a breakthrough. "At the time I didn't have a great deal going and yet I felt that I was capable of being very successful," he says. "She kept pushing and said, 'You can!' It was very important for me to be able to do it for her as well as for myself."

They were married in 1977. After the birth of their son Christopher Cody, they started spending more time on a 1,200-acre farm in Marianne's home state of Georgia, where Rogers bred Arabian horses and cattle and drove a tractor. "That's what this country is all about," says Rogers, whose grandfather was a small farmer. With the ranch up for sale for $11 million, Rogers is living in Bel Air and plans to build another home on land he purchased in the Hollywood Hills.

With wife Marianne

Emma Samms

Emma Samms's plans for a dance career were dashed by a hip injury at age sixteen that threatened to cripple her. But the setback took Emma on a new course: the twenty-six-year-old London-born actress found her life changed overnight when she started playing torrid love scenes with soap's most popular leading men. She landed the role of Holly Sutton on "General Hospital" and became the woman who made Luke forget Laura. Her tempestuous onscreen marriage to Robert Scorpio, played by Australian heartthrob Tristan Rogers, developed into a real-life love affair. Emma's fast-rising career tipped her into the superstar world of "Dynasty" as Fallon, the wife of Jeff Colby. The girl who had dreamed of following in her mother's footsteps as a ballerina was on her way to stardom as a steamy actress in the most-watched TV show in the world.

Joan Collins

One of television's richest actresses, Joan Collins, once stood in line at the unemployment office. She faced a mid-life crisis as an out-of-work actress with a family to feed. That's just one chapter in Joan's racy life, filled with tempestuous romances with moguls and superstars, which she candidly confessed in her autobiography, *Past Imperfect.* Today Joan wears expensive clothes, travels by limousine, and enjoys life's finest luxury, thanks to her incredible popularity as TV's number one vixen—the sexy evil "Dynasty" character Alexis Carrington Colby.

Her $3 million-plus salary is just the tip of the iceberg, which melts down to millions more in royalties from her massive merchandising deals. Joan has a financial stake in the phenomenal industry that's grown up around "Dynasty," marketing everything from $10 tights to $250,000 fur coats. She's the magic draw behind perfume, luggage, dolls, jewelry, and home furnishings. The English actress who was destitute nine years ago now lives in a towering mansion with an Olympic-sized swimming pool off Beverly Hills' Coldwater Canyon. Decorated in a combination of art deco and English country style, it has ersatz silver palm trees and a lounge bar, where the walls are covered with over fifty magazine covers of Joan.

The younger of her two daughters, Katie, age thirteen, lives with her. In the lowest point of Joan's roller-coaster life, Katie battled for survival after a near-fatal car accident in England in 1980, but miraculously recovered her full health. After three failed marriages, including one to British pop star Tony Newley, Joan values her independence. But romance is still very much alive for Joan, who has found love again with a handsome Swede, Peter Holm, fourteen years her junior.

*Left: Roger Moore and Sean Connery.
Below: Larry Hagman. Right: John
Forsythe and Linda Evans*

Sophia Loren

Her extraordinary beauty has placed her in the pantheon of the world's most celebrated women. The incomparable Sophia Loren remains the reigning queen of the European superstars. She has starred in more than fifty films, including the Oscar-winning *Two Women* in 1961, and her rags-to-riches story is legendary.

Despite her success and all its trappings, Sophia's greatest joy came with motherhood. She has two sons with her husband, film director Carlo Ponti—Carlo Jr., age sixteen, and Edoardo, who at age twelve costarred with his famous mother in the TV film *Aurora*. Her boys share her magnificent secluded villa in Geneva, Switzerland, with its chandeliers and marbled rooms —an elegant hideaway that gives them privacy together.

Sophia's beauty has only increased over the years—so much so that her words of wisdom on the subject became a best-selling book, *Women and Beauty*. An entire cottage industry rests on her charisma —a line of eyewear, cosmetics, and promotion for a Florida resort. She is spending more time in the United States since she bought a California farm. She sums up her philosophy of beauty this way: "For me beauty is harmony. There is no harmony in your body if it's not with your mental qualities."

With son Edoardo (left)

COLLECTIONS

Tom Barrett

He's the country's foremost collector and broker of antique, vintage, and classic cars. He's the founder of the world-famous Scottsdale, Arizona, auction which brings in millions of dollars in sales a year.

He jokingly refers to himself as "a used car salesman," but Tom Barrett is a car dealer extraordinaire, a man who has owned many of the rare blue-blooded cars in circulation. They include cars that once belonged to movie stars and world figures, like Mussolini, Haile Selassie, and the Shah of Iran, whose Phantom IV is the biggest Rolls-Royce convertible ever built, valued at $350,000 today. There's also the Mercedes Hitler gave Stalin in 1939 to commemorate their nonaggression pact, valued at $1 million.

His lavish $2-million desert oasis in Arizona has vast garages filled to the limit with priceless cars. His personal favorite "keepers" include a Duesenberg, a Mercedes Roadster, a Bugatti, a V-16 Cadillac, and a Brewster-bodied Rolls-Royce. At fifty-six, Barrett has been buying and selling exotic autos for more than four decades. His clients are kings, movie stars, entrepreneurs, and regular Joes with a passion for cars—and a good deal of cold cash on hand. "Nine out of ten times, it's all cash; they write you a check," he says. "If you've got into this top echelon and you're going to finance one of these automobiles, I don't think you belong in it."

Château de Thoiry

. . . .

The Vicomte Paul de la Panouse
and his American-born wife,
Vicomtesse Annabelle, reside in the
spectacular Château de Thoiry—a
historic sixteenth-century castle
twenty-five miles west of Paris. The
stately historic monument, on 1,200
acres of French gardens, has been
in the Vicomte's family for 400
years and is filled with impressive
treasures.

Centuries of taxes and shortage
of labor have made the cost of
maintaining the castle a crippling
expense. So in 1967 the Vicomte
took $3 million from the dwindling
ancestral savings and created the
Château de Thoiry African Game
Reserve on the vast acreage of his
property. The Vicomte, a lover of
African fauna and a student of zo-
ology, imported more than 1,000
exotic animals, including lions, ele-
phants, zebras, tigers, camels, and
many rare endangered species to
attract money-paying visitors.

Annabelle, a real-life Cinderella
from Wasoda, Minnesota, relates
how she met her handsome prince
at a restaurant in Paris when she
was a model: "He reached into his
pocket and pulled out his card and
said: 'Here, mademoiselle, take my
card—and the next time you're in
Paris, do call me and come and see
my lions.' Which I thought was the
best line I'd ever heard!"

The Vatican

Millions of people come to the Vatican in Rome every year to stand on the holy ground and perhaps get a glimpse of the Pope, as did Linda Evans. The Vatican museums house the world's biggest collection of classical art. These treasures represent the combined artistic achievement of humanity and their value is beyond price.

The Popes have historically been the world's greatest patrons of art, commissioning artists such as Rosselli, Botticelli, Raphael, and Michelangelo to adorn the Vatican with their works. When Pope Julius II asked Michelangelo to paint the ceiling of the Sistine Chapel, the artist spent four years suspended on a mattress, creating nine tableaux depicting the creation of the universe and man.

The first great works in the Vatican art collection were placed in the Belvedere Pavilion. It now houses many invaluable masterpieces, such as the *Apollo Belvedere* pictured here, which was one of the ancient statues placed there by Julius II.

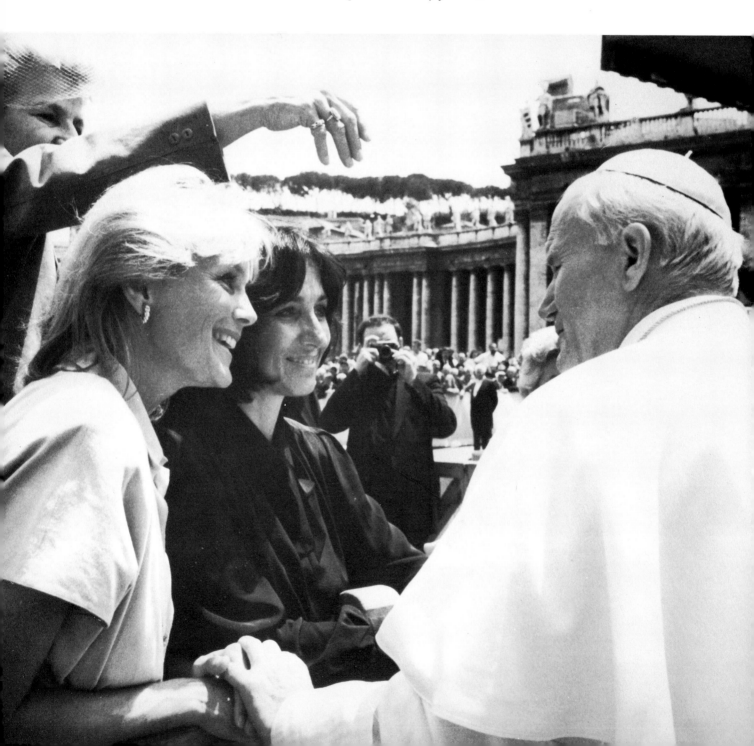

Dr. Lonnie Hammargren

If a man's home is his castle, then neurosurgeon Dr. Lonnie Hammargren's creation is his living fantasy. Many top doctors can relax in their own private hot tubs, but who would think of using a real NASA space capsule to shade himself from the blazing Las Vegas desert sun in his backyard Jacuzzi? That's only one wacky possession belonging to this skilled doctor and zany collector.

He has an instant cure for boredom, taking aerial trips on Gary Wells's old stunt cycle on a monorail track suspended over his swimming pool. Hammargren, unlike other bike enthusiasts, collects wrecks. His house is filled with offbeat bric-à-brac he's collected from all over the world and each room is modeled on a different country. A subterranean Egyptian tomb garages some of his rare automobile collection, including his prized Bugatti, designed for the 1936 Paris Auto Show. But one of his most unique cars is a 1936 wood-bodied Rolls-Royce, built as a British military vehicle. To test its watertightness, the good doctor drove it into a lake for a lark—but the stunt put the car back into the shop with a flooded exhaust.

Dr. Hammargren's passion for the unusual started with the building of his controversial observatory, which upset his affluent neighbors. He's created a private planetarium inside his house. "My interests are not in the mainstream," he says. "It's just that I've had the courage to carry out and execute some of the fantasies people have."

Sotheby's

. . . .

Sotheby's Fine Art Auction is the ultimate candy store for rich and famous collectors. The bidding is fierce for fine art aficionados, who might pick up an impressionist masterpiece. This Edgar Degas painting, *Au Musée du Louvre,* fetched $2.53 million at a Sotheby's sale in 1984.

The highest price paid for a work of contemporary art at Sotheby's was $1.65 million for a painting by Mark Rothko. For slightly higher than that price, one buyer added a suit of armor to his closet. A Louis VI French cabinet went for a mere $1.4 million.

But even at Sotheby's, where talk in millions comes easy, they still speak in hushed tones over one item that fetched the highest price in their 240-year history. It was $11.9 million for the twelfth-century biblical manuscript the Gospels of Henry the Lion—sold to the West German government.

Fabergé Eggs

Malcolm Forbes, the magazine publisher, added this bejeweled cuckoo egg to his collection of fabled Fabergé Easter eggs last year. He paid $1.76 million for the exquisite piece at a Sotheby's auction.

The highly sought, magnificent Easter eggs, made in Imperial Russia for the Czars by jeweler extraordinaire Carl Fabergé, represent the crowning achievement of the goldsmith's art. The cuckoo egg, eight inches high and encrusted with gold filigree and pearls, is one of only fifty-four that were made by the Russian goldsmith for the imperial family.

Mr. Forbes has assiduously purchased most of the eggs known to remain in private hands and has them on exhibition at the Forbes Museum in Manhattan. Each of the eggs contains a surprise miniature inside. At the press of a button, a gold grill at the top of the cuckoo egg flips open and a tiny rooster, decorated with feathers, emerges in song. The egg was presented by Czar Nicholas II to his wife, the Empress Alexandra Fedorovna, in 1900.

MULTIMILLIONAIRES

Malcolm Forbes

He's the king of the "Capitalist Tool Empire"—the slogan and the success behind *Forbes* magazine—a $200-million business of which Malcolm Forbes is the sole shareholder.

His father's thrifty Scottish philosophy was waste not want not, while his mother loved to spend. When Forbes inherited the magazine, you might say he took after his mother. Let's start with his sixty-eight motorcycles. He loves to share these rich boy's toys with his friends and employees on club runs all over the countryside. A few years ago, Forbes and his "Capitalist Tools" trumpeted the virtues of free enterprise on a 1,500-mile trip across China by motorcycle and in one of the eight famous Forbes hot air balloons.

The Forbes balloons are a promotional stunt that match his high-flying lifestyle. Each year he celebrates with an international balloon meet at his seventeenth-century château in Balleroy, France. The *pièce de résistance* is Forbes's château balloon, a replica of his Normandy château—his very own castle in the sky, created for a mere million. Forbes owns seven homes with his wife Bertie and their five children. "The Capitalist Tool" 727 flies them to their Moroccan palace in Tangier, their fishing village in Tahiti, their Christopher Wren-designed London townhouse, their ranches in Wyoming and Colorado, or their very own Fijian island of 350 acres. Their chief home is Fair Hills, New Jersey.

"Those that regard money as a crushing responsibility don't usually manage to hang onto it," he says. "I'm going to be a long time dead, so I'd rather get the maximum while living, on the premise that on the next trip, I might not have it as good."

Adnan Khashoggi

While America's richest man, Sam Walton, has $2.8 billion, the flamboyant Saudi mega-mogul Adnan Khashoggi, is estimated to have more than $10 billion. One Khashoggi deal can affect stock markets, governments, and corporations right across the face of the earth. His multimillion-dollar transactions, his $2.5-billion divorce case, the stars and celebrities he entertains lavishly in his thirty-five family homes, all have splashed Khashoggi across international headlines and only added to the mystique of this globe-trotting Midas known as "The Chief."

I was invited to celebrate Khashoggi's fiftieth birthday in the summer of 1985 at his Spanish mountaintop estate above the international playground of Marbella. For the lavish nonstop five-day party, Khashoggi had built a special dining pavilion to accommodate six hundred of his closest friends, including the cream of European aristocracy. Khashoggi usually choppers into his 13,000-acre La Baraka estate, with eight villas for himself and his seven children. This is just a handy hunting lodge where the family can shoot from his reserve of fifteen hundred wild goats and mountain elk and seventy thousand pheasants. His unbridled pride and joy are the thirty priceless Cairo thoroughbred Arabian stallions, kept there in top condition by a team of trainers.

Khashoggi's 325-foot yacht, the *Nabilia,* named for his only daughter, was moored in Marbella Bay. Its engineering rivals any naval destroyer on the seas, with its own helicopter, hospital, movie theater, disco, and eleven VIP suites, each named after a precious jewel. But true to form, Khashoggi hopes to sell the *Nabilia*

With wife Lamia at Khashoggi's fiftieth birthday celebration in Marbella, Spain

for $100 million to build an even bigger yacht—complete with its own seven-passenger submarine, his and hers helicopter pads, room for four Rolls-Royces, and surface-to-air missiles.

Khashoggi spends one hundred hours a month aboard his private DC-8, clocking nearly three-quarters of a million miles a year. The plane "puts Air Force One to shame," according to a former presidential aide who was a passenger. Khashoggi has dubbed it *2001*. With a full-time entourage, including a chiropractor, the annual cost of this high-flying life is $50 million, not including fuel.

When Khashoggi's feet touch the ground, he can choose to stay at a string of thirty-five spectacular homes, from a villa in the Canary Islands to a 15,000-acre ranch in Kenya, complete with lions, a crocodile pit, rare birds, and a resident African tribe. In New York, his Fifth Avenue Olympic Towers home is actually sixteen separate apartments on two floors—the largest and most expensive single apartment in the world, with a price tag of $25 million. Features include a swimming pool and Jacuzzi, both with views, a $200,000 Russian sable bedspread, and a $30-million art collection.

For Adnan Khashoggi, life is a huge Monopoly game. The heritage may be Arabic, but his philosophy is all-American, free enterprise to the glittering core.

Interior of Khashoggi private plane (above right);
Khashoggi, Yvette Mimieux, and Lamia (below)

Malcolm Forbes's balloons at Château de Balleroy, France

Donald Trump

Donald Trump has put his imprint on the golden rock of Manhattan as the head of a billion-dollar real estate empire. "I don't believe anyone has built more things than we have," says the blond, blue-eyed six-footer, whose grandiose schemes have single-handedly changed the skyline of New York. Trump's conservative blue business suits and black chauffeured limousine belie his brash flair for business. "I believe in spending extra money," he says. "I believe in spending maybe more money than other people would think almost rational."

Trump's money-is-no-object credo is apparent in the 1,400-room Grand Hyatt Hotel and in his $500-million projects in Atlantic City, including Trump's Castle, one of the largest casino-hotels in the world, and Trump Plaza, a $125-million cooperative housing complex. "I'd rather spend the ultimate dollars and have the ultimate place," says the forty-year-old tycoon. His trump card is a sixty-eight-story office and apartment complex on Fifth Avenue, with a six-floor atrium, housing some of the world's most elegant stores, which have to turn over a million dollars a year just to pay the rent. The pink-mirrored, marbled Trump Tower, with cascading plants and a waterfall and a grand piano downstairs, is home to celebrities and millionaires, including Johnny Carson, Paul Anka, Steven Spielberg, Sophia Loren, and Martina Navratilova. Apartments start at $600,000 and go up to $10 million for triplexes on the top few floors.

Trump and his Austrian-Czech wife Ivana occupy penthouse floors there. Ivana, an interior designer who works with Trump on his projects, found them a charming Connecticut country estate with fourteen bedrooms, eighteen bathrooms, and a dining room large enough to be a chic bistro. The 100-acre property has an underground bowling alley, a ten-car garage, and comes with its own island. The price tag: $10 million. For relaxation this high roller doesn't just buy a ticket to the ball game—he sinks $10 million into buying an entire football team—the New Jersey Generals. Donald Trump—staking a fortune and having fun playing the game.

Meshulam Ricklis

The name Meshulam Ricklis is hardly a household word. But when you're a multimillionaire in control of fifty companies worth $1.5 billion, who really cares? Thirty years ago he revolutionized the way of doing business on Wall Street. He bought small undervalued companies and merged them as the first conglomerates. But it was an aspiring singer, Pia Zadora, who put the Ricklis fortune in the spotlight. In 1978, Ricklis, now sixty, married Pia, who is twenty-three years younger. He started bankrolling her to stardom at a cost estimated to be $10 million. Their jet-set lifestyle includes a private helicopter and two planes to fly them anywhere in the world and between their homes in New York and Los Angeles. "He's basically a farmer by nature," says Pia. "And that's the way his heart is. He'll iron my clothes and wash out my lingerie and cook for me and carry my makeup; things like that are duties of love that he doesn't mind doing. And he doesn't mind being called Mr. Zadora because he knows who he is."

With wife Pia Zadora

Richard Branson
· ·

England's multimillionaire music genius Richard Branson is flying high at age thirty-three as founder of Virgin Records and Virgin Airlines. Branson's supersonic career has taken off since he dropped out of school at age fifteen and started a mail-order record house. He called the company Virgin because he was young and innocent. Today the record company is worth over $200 million and boasts a list of artists that includes Boy George, Phil Collins, and Human League. In 1984 he launched the "discount flier" airline. His Virgin operations, based in the United Kingdom, also include music and book publishing, a music cable channel aimed at Europe via satellite, recording studios, nightclubs, video, computer software, films, and record stores.

Creating a family environment is an integral part of Branson's philosophy. So at age seventeen, well before he made his first shilling from Boy George, Branson purchased a sixteenth-century mansion far from London. Once the estate of Charles I, this mansion now welcomes the kings of the music industry, who swim, play tennis, go-cart, and enjoy the grounds while recording there. On weekends Branson closes himself off from business at his cottage on the estate. It's not the fancy home you'd expect, but it provides a peaceful backdrop for raising a close family.

"I get my satisfaction from new ventures, new achievements," says Branson. "I'm personally not interested in big cars, clothes, gold watches—all the things that money can buy you on a personal basis." Branson runs his empire from a houseboat, which he bought for $150 at age sixteen. "Running the company from the boat is far more pleasant than running it from a suite of offices," he says.

HOMES

Jane Seymour

English beauty Jane Seymour has won fame for her steamy screen performances. She's bewitched a succession of leading men, including Roger Moore, Christopher Reeve, and Tom Selleck. But in real life she's a genteel lady of the manor and her country squire is husband and business manager David Flynn, with whom she has two children. For Jane, age thirty-three, it is her third marriage and she's finally found her greatest happiness in the privacy of her own home with her family.

She balances her transatlantic lifestyle between a French provincial house in Beverly Hills and a thousand-year-old manor house in England, which sits in a valley in Cotswolds. Jane's estate, dating back to Elizabethan times, includes a church, two cottages, and a tithe barn. "There's nothing like getting down to grass roots," says Jane. "It's a place we run away to. It's a place where our children can run wild and free and I can run wild and free."

While in England, Jane loves to ride, scour antique shops, and devote time to her daughter's piano playing and swimming. "I'm one of the few British people who are very happy in America and part of that happiness is that we have a place in England and we go back frequently. So I feel we have two different lives."

Michele Lee

For Michele Lee, work doesn't stop when she leaves the "Knots Landing" set and steps out of her character as Karen Fairgate MacKenzie. In her time away from the studio, Michele spearheads an entertainment industry antidrug campaign, work which has helped her form a strong friendship with former First Lady Betty Ford, who has won her own battle with alcohol addiction.

Divorced from actor James Farentino, Michele is a devoted mother to their fifteen-year-old son David, despite her hectic schedule. "This house is totally a reflection of me," she says of the home she bought in 1970. "I did everything myself. I love decorating. I guess it's part of an expression of who Michele Lee is." Here she spends time alone in her bedroom, studying scripts and unwinding, or singing to the strains of her computer piano.

"I'm really a homebody," Michele says. "I enjoy nice things. I've worked very hard over many, many years and that's the really nice part —being able to reap some of the good stuff from it." The Mediterranean-style house, decorated with lovely furnishings Michele has picked up at antique stores, bargain boutiques, and estate sales, is not big—three bedrooms and a den. But the rooms are spacious and overflowing with pieces that blend together beautifully. "When you take the time to handpick things, you're handpicking memories you can hold onto, no matter what."

Bobby Vinton

This $7-million Mediterranean villa overlooking the Pacific Ocean was once inhabited by Hollywood's royalty. The magnificent mansion was home for Douglas Fairbanks, Jr., David O. Selznick, and Cary Grant. Today this once-neglected hilltop palace has been carefully restored to its former regal splendor by the son of a Polish bandleader who became a prince—Bobby Vinton.

When he first stepped foot inside the house, he felt a strong connection to its historic past. He walked into the library and opened the bookcases to the mansion's secret passageway. Somehow he knew it was there without ever being told.

"They said, 'How did you know about the passage? Nobody's been in this house and knows these things,'" recalls Vinton. "I really felt at home here for the first time. I mean, I came back to where I belong and this is where I'd always been."

Engelbert Humperdinck

As a struggling singer called Gerry Dorsey, playing local workingmen's clubs in England, he was so poor he had to sleep in phone booths and at railway stations. Today the pub singer, who changed his name to Engelbert Humperdinck, is a multimillionaire earning a colossal $300,000 a week in Las Vegas and can choose to bed down at any one of his five mansions—from Las Vegas to Beverly Hills to a swanky suburb of London.

The Beverly Hills mansion he really calls home was formerly owned by sex goddess Jayne Mansfield and reflects the opulence of Hollywood's golden era. It's filled with antiques, oil paintings, and statues Humperdinck has collected around the world. No longer all-pink, as in Jayne's day, the home still has the famous heart-shaped swimming pool created especially for her. But more than just memories of Jayne remain. Humperdinck claims he and his wife have seen Jayne Mansfield's ghost.

The walls of Humperdinck's den are covered with his forty gold and eight platinum records. But the forty-seven-year-old superstar's favorite room is the seventy-five-foot-long parlor, with beamed ceilings and his most prized possession—the piano on which George Gershwin composed *Rhapsody in Blue.*

Two of Humperdinck's four teenagers live with him in America, while the others are studying in England and living with his wife, who's always preferred to live in their native land. But distance is no obstacle for the globe-trotting "Mr. Romance," who logs four hundred thousand miles a year. On the ground, he has a fleet of Rolls-Royces, including the largest manufactured, a Phantom VI, as well as a 1964 Bentley and a Cadillac Eldorado Classic convertible.

Robert Vaughn

· ·

Winterland is the three-story home of actor Robert Vaughn and his wife Linda. The Vaughns restored the classic twenty-three-room mansion in Ridgefield, Connecticut, and priced it for sale at $2 million. Vaughn notes the Houdini family once owned it. It was built in 1905 by America's last ambassador to the Czar of Russia after he returned from diplomatic service. At one stage the Catholic Church owned it and sixty-five monks held services in the ballroom.

"It's only seven acres, a lot by Beverly Hills standards, but it's not a lot on the East Coast," says Vaughn. "There aren't any houses near here, so we

actually can look for miles and miles. You can see three states from the widow's walk."

Vaughn traded his Solo lifestyle as a bachelor Hollywood actor-about-town, best known for "The Man from U.N.C.L.E.," and finally got married at age forty-one in 1974 to actress Linda. They have a son, Cassidy, and daughter, Caitlin.

"Linda is a remarkable decorator and restorer," says Vaughn. "We both love homes; we love decorating them, we love restoring them, and we love moving around. I'm sure we'll always be buying different houses, different homes, and moving around for the rest of our lives. The hub of our life is always our home."

John Lennon and Yoko Ono, Palm Beach Home

. . . .

This luxurious seafront mansion in Palm Beach, Florida, is where rock legend and superstar John Lennon came to get away from it all. It was in the airy music room here that the famous Beatle composed many of his later solo works. This dream palace was lovingly restored but kept true to its original Spanish design, with artful stone and tile work, classically sculpted windows, and a secluded pool. Lennon's widow, Yoko Ono, put the house of poignant memories on the market. The price tag: $8 million.

Jaclyn Smith

Home and family have always come first for green-eyed Texas beauty Jaclyn Smith. Away from the cameras and popping flashbulbs, the former top model whose career took off as one of the original "Charlie's Angels" finds her greatest fulfillment behind the doors of her antique-filled Bel Air house with her third husband, British cameraman Tony Richmond, and their four-year-old son Gaston.

"I am really all about marriage, family, and home," she says. "A lot of my dreams for happiness and a baby have come completely true with Tony. I am the happiest I have ever been in my life—completely content and at peace."

Her current home, which she's lovingly furnished, is the center of her existence. She prefers to give small dinners in her classically elegant but warm dining room, rather than go out in public. One of her most prized possessions is the canopied brass bed in the bedroom—a piece that once reposed in a palace. It was among the first antique pieces she ever bought and she paid it off in installments for six months. Jaclyn Smith—keeping the home fires burning.

Bob Guccione

. . . .

Penthouse magazine publisher Bob Guccione lives in a palatial 28,000-square-foot double townhouse in New York's fashionable East Side, just steps from Fifth Avenue, with enough art to fill a museum—Botticelli, Bellini, Modigliani, Picasso, Matisse, and Chagall. The house, which he shares with longtime business associate, friend, and true love Kathy Keeton, has a Mediterranean ambiance—white Carrara marble floors, Venetian mirrors, and carved antique furniture.

Guccione and Keeton struggled desperately in the early days to put out their magazine and were so poor they "borrowed" milk bottles off people's doorsteps for their breakfast. Today Keeton's bathroom boasts twenty-four-karat gold tiles, a Jacuzzi, white marble columns, and a Picasso over the tub. There's a swimming pool surrounded by marble statues, a projection room, exercise room, sauna, and a time capsule buried in the garden, filled with predictions. They own the hand-carved gold-leaf piano that belonged to Judy Garland. What could be more fitting to guard the gold tiles, gold piano, and priceless art collection than a dog with a solid-gold fang—just one of the Rhodesian Ridgeback hunting dogs that protect the mansion?

"We decided when we designed the house that we wanted something so complete that if we chose never to go out again, we wouldn't miss the outside world," says Guccione. "And frankly, that's what we've done here."

Cher

Superstar actress and entertainer Cher is "Cleopatra of Hollywood" in her sumptuous thirteen-bedroom, six-bathroom mansion, custom-built to suit her highly individual style. Four years in the planning, Cher reached back to ancient Egypt for the decor, borrowing from the monumental lines of the Sphinx. The three-story atrium has a lounge full of Egyptian art and a dining area. Her movie star pool makes other Hollywood swimming holes look shabby and she has a gym equipped with state-of-the-art equipment to maintain her lithe form for her trademark risqué gowns, which are hung in a series of dressing rooms.

Cher's daughter Chastity and son Elisha have their own designer bedrooms upstairs, where the hall walls display her favorite Indian jewelry. Her bedroom is a Moroccan-themed fantasy chamber with shimmering black and gold, a four-poster bed, magnificent fireplace, and views over the California hills. The bathroom has a huge sunken tub, befitting a queen of the Nile. Cher priced her exotic mansion for sale at $6.5 million.

Jane Seymour with husband David Flynn and daughter

Liberace

Liberace is known around the world as "Mr. Showmanship" for his candelabra trademark and his millions earned as a performer with his thousand-megawatt smile and dazzling costumes. The boy who started playing the piano at four years old grew up poor in Milwaukee, and wore hand-me-down clothes. Today he lives lavishly and thinks nothing of dropping $350,000 on one fur coat. He's spent fortunes creating opulent environments in his spectacular Las Vegas and Palm Springs homes.

Liberace owns some of the world's most priceless antiques and wherever he travels he goes on adding to his overflowing treasure collection. If he can't buy it, he commissions it—like the knockoff Sistine Chapel ceiling in his Las Vegas bedroom. Liberace imported an Italian mural painter who worked, Michelangelo-style, for six months to create the frescoes.

His treasures include Chopin's piano and a miniature diamond piano valued at well over $10 million. Even though he added room after room to his home, he ran out of space. So he built a museum and filled that too. Fans by the thousand visit to see his extravagant cars, memorabilia, and personal antiques, such as Napoleon and Josephine's famous china set, worth almost $200,000. Even Liberace doesn't serve tea on that. Liberace —one of the world's richest stars, living a dream.

Robert Stack

Robert Stack and his wife Rosemary have lived in their beautiful Bel Air, California, mansion for twenty-five years, ever since they were married. The veteran Hollywood actor says of his home, "It really is, for me at least, a sanctum. The profession that we're in makes you so vulnerable and you're up there for grabs. Your show has been dropped or picked up or they love you or they hate you. Here you can close the gates or close the front door and there is your little parameter in which you live— emotionally and everything else."

Stack is a sportsman who was a world-class skeet-shooting champion at sixteen years old and used to shoot with Gable, Hemingway, and Howard Hughes. His gun collection hangs on a wall of his den, where he also has sports trophies on display for polo, boat racing, and shooting. The Stack home, with its tennis court and swimming pool, is also an ideal place for entertaining, with an indoor-outdoor feeling, suitable for elegant small dinners or informal get-togethers. "You can put your feet up, you can open it up and you can entertain outdoors," he says. "In California you can have two hundred people around a pool. If the party's boring, just push 'em in the pool. It works very nicely. It's casual, yet you can make it as formal as you want."

Siegfried and Roy

. . . .

A unique blending of magic and illusion with the drama of wild jungle beasts have made Siegfried and Roy one of the highest-paid acts in Las Vegas. The German-born twosome has performed their magic in Las Vegas for over ten years at the Frontier Hotel.

Their home in the desert resort is a Garden of Eden for them and their rare collection of wild animals. Five years in the making, the house cost over $10 million. They put in eighty-five palm trees and made the grounds lush for the lions and other animals to roam freely. It's an environment fit for the king of the jungle, where the beasts have their own swimming pool and waterfall to cool off during the Las Vegas heat. Their prize possessions are their two white tiger cubs and an extremely rare snow-white tiger. There is also a Lippizaner stallion, a goat, several macaws, four Great Danes, and a not-so-ferocious cat.

Siegfried and Roy's jungle palace is filled with objects from their worldwide travels. They have a mystical communion with their animals. They live, work, and play together as a family. It's not unusual to find a black panther in the bathroom or a lion in front of the TV set. "What we really had in mind was to create an oasis for us," says Roy. "We make the animals feel at home. They're part of our surroundings." Even when the performers are on the road, their thoughts are never far from home: "Wherever our travels take us, we call home every day because the animals miss us that much—and we miss knowing how they are doing."

Hugh Hefner

Playboy publisher Hugh Hefner has fully lived up to the name of the $200-million empire he created. The key to that pleasure-seeking mystique leads behind the doors of the Playboy Mansion in Los Angeles, the West Coast headquarters of his company's activities—and the home that is the scene of his legendary parties.

Hefner moved West in 1971 from the fabulous forty-eight-room Playboy Mansion in Chicago, setting up his bunny hutch on five and a half acres in exclusive Holmby Hills. The elegant Tudor-style house sits in handsomely landscaped grounds, with a tennis court, swimming pool, ponds, waterfalls, and exotic varieties of fish, birds, and animals. Flamingos, cranes, and peacocks strut through the grounds. Parrots and other tropical birds, including ostriches and condors, flit around.

Hefner can indulge his obsession for games in the game house, which is filled with pinball machines. There are guest houses and a greenhouse. His favorite area is his bedroom, where his large rectangular bed is surrounded by an array of electronic gear and video equipment.

The most popular spot on the estate is the grotto he built as part of the pool, which can be entered by swimming through a waterfall—and includes an elaborate series of Jacuzzi baths that are a center of social activity. "The rumor is that you don't age when you're on the property," says Hefner. "I think there's some truth to that."

TRANSPORTATION

Orient Express

. . . .

The Orient Express revives an era of luxury train travel and international intrigue. Today's jet-set celebrities and wealthy travelers know that getting there is more than half the fun and they're willing to pay top dollar for a nostalgic journey to the world's great cities —London, Paris, Venice, Vienna, Istanbul. "Lifestyles" caught up with actresses Morgan Fairchild and Jennifer O'Neill, who joined a roster of stars including Liza Minnelli and Cher who've traveled on the train of kings and king of trains.

For nine decades, following its maiden voyage in 1883, the Orient Express carried diplomats, royalty, smugglers, lovers, and spies between Paris and Istanbul. Apathy and air travel derailed the legendary train in 1972, but wealthy backers put it back on the tracks again ten years and $20 million later, with the antique cars lovingly restored to their original splendor of inlaid ivory woods and gleaming brass. The moving palace has elegant teak and mahogany dining cars, where the finest cuisine is served at candlelit tables with Lalique crystal. Morgan and Jennifer stepped aboard for a champagne journey in the style of a bygone age.

Inset: Morgan Fairchild (left) and Jennifer O'Neill.

Regent Air

When did your favorite airline last offer you a bed with fine Irish linen sheets? And do you always get Dom Perignon champagne before and after takeoff? In the era of no-frills flying, Regent Air is charting a different course. Passengers on the exclusive coast-to-coast airline live high as they fly high amid the lavish art deco splendor of Regent's 727 jets. Bicoastal executives now have a luxury alternative to red-eye flights from New York to Los Angeles and can fly in style, surrounded by all the corporate comforts of home: four conference rooms, secretarial service, air-to-ground telephone, market reports, private landing and takeoff areas, and limousine service to and from Regent's private terminals. There's even an airborne hairdresser and bar service and entertainment in the central lounge and dining room. Meals are served on elegant Spode china and Regent's private compartments have queen-sized beds. But nobody who is rich and famous blinks at the prices.

Elvis Presley's Jet

When it came to extravagance, the sky was the limit for Elvis Presley and his ultimate toy was this Convair 880 passenger jet, which he bought in 1975 and named for his daughter Lisa Marie.

It wasn't unusual for him to spend $5,000 to take friends up for a spin over his Graceland mansion and in 1976 alone he spent $400,000 on fuel. Elvis spent twenty days a month in this lavish penthouse in the clouds during the last years of his life, lounging on the lush blue velvet sofa listening to the plane's quadraphonic stereo system or playing backgammon in the airborne conference room on his way to Las Vegas. The plane's two bathrooms had gold-plated fixtures.

Shortly after his death, the jetliner was sold for $1.5 million, but six years later the *Lisa Marie* returned home to Memphis, where it sits across the road from Graceland, a nostalgic showpiece for thousands of fans.

Super-Luxury Production Cars

Rolls-Royce—the name is the ultimate symbol of class and expensive taste in automobile production. The most valuable Rolls is the famous 1907 Silver Ghost—so-named because its metal parts were silver-plated and because of its extraordinary silence. There is only one Silver Ghost—although Rolls-Royce built a 40–50 horsepower Ghost model until 1925. The historic Silver Ghost is still on the road today in the U.S., with more than a half a million miles on the odometer. The British company has turned down an offer of $2 million for it.

The ultimate Rolls-Royce made today is the Silver Spur—only twelve were introduced into the U.S. last year. The price tag of $185,000 makes it the most expensive production car built today. The runner-up is the Aston Martin Lagonda—only sixty are available in the U.S. each year. The no-frills price is a mere $160,000, but customizing can run the cost up to almost a quarter of a million dollars. Get yours while they last!

Aston Martin Lagonda (above left); Rolls-Royce Silver Spur (below left); Rolls-Royce Silver Ghost (above).

QE 2

Her Royal Highness of the high seas, the *Queen Elizabeth 2,* has steamed over two million miles since her maiden voyage in 1968. Along that course, the *QE 2* has adorned the world's most exciting ports and pampered a long list of celebrity travelers.

In an era of supersonic travel, you can fly from New York to England in just three hours on the Concorde. But when it comes to quality time, wealthy travelers prefer to take to the high seas in the ultimate luxury, making the five-day trip in the *QE 2*'s super-deluxe Queen Mary and Queen Elizabeth four-person suites for a total cost of $24,250. For that price, they travel with their own private veranda for ocean viewing, king-sized beds, eight-foot-long suede sofa, bar, stereo, VCR, and a Jacuzzi with gold-plated bath fixtures. For those with money and time to burn, there's the *QE 2*'s ninety-five-day round-the-world cruise, with ultra-luxury suite accommodation at $325,000.

You can indulge in champagne and caviar buffets, relax in the indoor and outdoor pools or health spa, or browse the glittering shopping arcade, where you might easily spend more than the cost of a high-priced ticket, as "Lifestyles'" guest Lee Meredith discovered. This floating millionaire's city even boasts an offshore branch of London's posh Harrods department store.

John Lennon's Bentley

. . . .

This relic of the psychedelic sixties era is the 1956 Bentley once owned by the late John Lennon, with its far-out paint job, pink shag carpeting, purple leather seats, paisley curtains, and an abundance of history. Shortly after Lennon's tragic death, it sold at an auction in Auburn, Indiana, for $350,000—a world record at that time.

But in June 1985 at Sotheby's in New York, the bids broke all records for a psychedelic yellow Rolls-Royce Phantom V owned by John Lennon in which the Beatles toured from 1966 to 1969. Bidding went up in $10,000 increments before Jim Pattison, chairman of Vancouver's Expo 1986, drove away the historic rock auto. The final price was $2.3 million.

Drive-a-Dream

Her clientele includes Michael Jackson, John Travolta, Roger Moore, Liza Minnelli, Eddie Murphy, Diana Ross, Elton John, and Douglas Fairbanks, Jr. Margaux Mirkin is heiress to the vast Budget Rent-a-Car fortune and she's brought new meaning to the word "budget" with her Beverly Hills-based Drive-a-Dream division of the company. The wealthy, royalty, and just plain folks pay $400 plus a day to drive rare and exotic cars. The twenty-seven-year-old entrepreneur's car showroom offers some of the rarest, most extravagant autos, selling for up to $300,000. Now she's moved into renting Lear jets at $1,000 an hour and offering helicopter dining at $500 an hour for lunch on the run above the hectic L.A. freeways. Business is booming because, as Margaux says, "In Los Angeles, you are what you ride and you are what you fly."

Robert Stigwood's Yacht

Music and movie mogul Robert Stigwood runs his multimillion-dollar empire from one of the grandest mobile offices in the world—his $20-million, 280-foot yacht, the *Jezebel.* Here he entertains guests including Elton John, Rod Stewart, and the Bee Gees in a sprawling living room with a grand piano, serving drinks from the yacht's French wine cellar. The yacht has a Jacuzzi, sauna, and steam room, a pine-paneled library, grand dining salon, seven staterooms, two working fireplaces, and wall-to-wall silk carpeting.

Stigwood, whose earnings from such films as *Saturday Night Fever, Tommy, Jesus Christ Superstar,* and *Grease* exceed $150 million, spotted the yacht on a Greek island and transformed it from a shabby relic to a seagoing palace, with a satellite communications system for making show business deals across the world.

Sea Goddess

Only the privileged elite can afford the ultimate cruising experience on the exclusive *Sea Goddess*—a spectacular $35-million vessel with only one class—first class—for 116 guests. "Lifestyles" caught up with Loretta Swit on this magnificent superyacht, which ventures into select harbors restricted to larger ships—Portofino, Corfu, and Monte Carlo. Genie Francis cruised with "Lifestyles" to the romantic Caribbean ports of St. Marten, St. Croix, Antigua, and Guadeloupe, going ashore to taste the islands' rich colonial past.

In port there's wind surfing, snorkeling, sailing, or water skiing off the ship's rear deck. At night the atmosphere is one of an exclusive club, with banquets created with fresh produce culled by chefs from the colorful island markets each day, plus gambling casinos and fabulous nightclub entertainment. The gracious style of the *Sea Goddess* inspires romance and more than one impetuous couple has decided to marry while cruising, including actress Arlene Dahl and groom Mark Rosen, who were wed aboard ship in the middle of the Mediterranean.

The cost of a week on the world's most expensive cruise ship, adding airfare to Europe, can easily run a couple a tab nearing five figures to recapture the style of the golden age of sea travel.

SHOPPING

Gucci

The famous interlocking initials spell top quality and elegance. The Gucci company, renowned for fine leather goods, caters to a wide public, with merchandise ranging from $5 Gucci matches to extravagant baubles, including a $120,000, thirty-six-karat, diamond-studded golf ball.

You don't have to be rich and famous to own a pair of Gucci loafers, but don't go on a spending spree at Gucci's New York or Beverly Hills shops unless your pockets are well lined. An elite ten thousand customers qualify for the golden key to the most expensive and exclusive part of each store. Here you find trinkets that sell for a cool quarter of a million dollars. The walls are decorated with paintings by modern masters, including Picasso and Modigliani. Don't ask the price—they're part of Dr. Aldo Gucci's personal collection: not for sale.

Dr. Gucci, the hard-driving patriarch of the company, has taken his family business from the back streets of Florence to worldwide prestige. It's paid off for this seventy-year-old multimillionaire in a personal lifestyle befitting European aristocracy.

Rodeo Drive, Beverly Hills

The sidewalks are paved with gold on the ultimate shopping strip of the rich and famous: Rodeo Drive. The world's most expensive boutiques line the exclusive blocks of this billionaire's bazaar, where stars and moguls, movie producers and princes come to be seen and pay the premium prices for prestige designer labels. When this world-renowned street was relatively unknown twenty-five years ago, Greta Garbo snapped up property that is worth a fortune today.

Celebrity clientele pop into these high-priced stores to buy items like a $65 T-shirt or a $9,000 gown. Many of the gowns that light up the Academy Awards come from Giorgio's, one of the most famous retailers on Rodeo Drive, where clothing and fragrances can drive a customer's bill into orbit. It's all in a day's shopping on this boulevard of the sweet life.

Bijan

· ·

He's the designer for kings, presidents, top entertainment figures, sports celebrities, and heads of state. But even the most illustrious clients must make an appointment to shop at Bijan's sumptuous Beverly Hills showroom on Rodeo Drive or his $10-million New York showroom on Fifth Avenue. His business brings in over $12 million a year from a closely guarded list of the world's wealthiest customers.

A suit with twenty-four-karat gold pinstripes runs $11,500; a bulletproof chinchilla-lined jacket costs $27,000; and even a pair of boots will set you back $3,250. It's his flair for the unusual that has made this forty-four-year-old Iranian so successful. Nothing else quite compares with his men's perfume, packaged in Baccarat crystal for $1,500 for six ounces, and his exquisite $10,000 twenty-four-karat gold-and-leather .38-caliber revolver that comes signed and numbered in its own mink-lined case.

Chanel

Coco Chanel, a young milliner who built a fashion empire, lived in opulence above her Paris store. She was a renegade who left the world of high fashion with an inciteful admonishment: "Fashion passes; style remains."

The designer chosen to carry on that legacy is somewhat of a renegade himself—a man given to wearing business suits and a ponytail and carrying a fan. His name is Karl Lagerfeld. The collections he creates are a triumph, fulfilling his belief in luxury, lavishness, and feminity, while still emphasizing the Chanel trademark black-and-white designs. "In fashion the secret of success is to do the right thing at the right moment," says Lagerfeld, age forty-four, who constantly jets between homes in Rome, Monte Carlo, Paris, Switzerland, and Brittany. "Fashion is something quite opportunistic."

Star Stores

More celebrities than ever are refusing the whims of the capricious show business industry to dictate their own fortunes. Instead they're turning to old-fashioned retailing as a second job to guarantee a steadier paycheck. TV star Randi Oakes owns Down Home, a Los Angeles outlet for craft artists that sells everything from quilts to folk art. The wife of one of Hollywood's richest producers, Candy Spelling, has a gift shop specializing in those expensive items that celebrities can't resist, like a $100 crystal E.T. bought as a gift for Steven Spielberg.

Australian chart-buster Olivia Newton-John accents the goodies from her native land at Koala Blue on L.A.'s fashionable Melrose Avenue. Olivia and partner Pat Ferrar fly home on buying sprees twice a year, collecting fashions by top designers, including knitted sweaters for $500. The store carries newspapers, magazines, books, and puzzles. Taste treats include Vegemite, Billy Tea, candy bars, and a snack bar serving Down Under milkshakes, Aussie Steak Pie, Captain Cook's Salad, and special desserts.

Above: Olivia Newton-John with partner Pat Ferrar. Inset: Olivia with Dame Edna Everage, Dudley Moore, and Susan Anton at Koala Blue opening party.

Cerutti

In the glamorous and treacherous world of fashion, Nino Cerutti has balanced at the pinnacle for almost a decade. The Paris-based empire of fragrances and fashion rings in $150 million a year.

At age nineteen, Cerutti took over the family fabric business started by his grandfather in 1881 at a woolen mill in Biella, Italy. He vaulted the company into the world of men's and women's couture by showcasing his clothes at controversial events, where models parade as thirties gangsters with machine guns or appear in front of bars on a blocked-off Paris street. Cerutti's playboy lifestyle was as flamboyant as his work.

Retired from the fast lane at age fifty-five, the designer splits his week commuting between his design centers and homes in Paris and Italy.

Nino Cerutti (far right) and models.

Revillon Furs

Diamonds may be a girl's best friend, but monied sophisticates know it's furs that warm a woman's heart. For more than two centuries—starting with French nobility—Revillon has draped the world's most pampered women in luxurious skins. Today the company's worldwide operation produces the ultimate in fur allure. Top-of-the-line models include a white Woven Mink for $32,000, a Mink Rovalia for $54,000, or, for the lucky woman who can afford to wear the very best, a Russian Lynx for $175,000. The opulent procession of white minks, pictured here from the 1985 collection designed for Revillon by Caroline Herrera, are the answer to every woman's dream. And who wouldn't feel like a superstar, wrapped in this glamorous white fox coat with ermine-cut mink collar?

ROYALTY

Queen Noor and King Hussein of Jordan

Former Princeton University cheerleader Lisa Halaby never dreamed she would one day be Queen of Jordan. As Queen Noor, the wife of King Hussein of Jordan, the thirty-four-year-old Washington-born beauty lives in a palace, entertains royalty and distinguished world leaders, and travels the world with a glittering entourage.

Married for eight years, she is the mother of three children—Princes Hamzah and Hashim, six and four, and Princess Iman, three. The royal couple live in Nadwah Palace in a walled compound housing many government buildings on the Mountain of Palaces in Amman. The Queen, who studied architecture and urban planning, has renovated and redecorated the old three-story palace in a combination of Arab and Western styles. The family's getaway palace is on the Red Sea at Aqaba, where they receive guests in an aqua-marine room as cool as the sparkling sea outside the double french windows. Queen Noor is a keen horse-woman and she can choose from eighty Arabian horses at the King's stables five miles from the center of Amman.

She met Hussein in 1976 on her first visit to Jordan, where she worked as coordinator of design for Alia airlines. He is sixteen years her senior, twice divorced and once widowed, and the father of seven children. He has been King since age seventeen.

Queen Noor has made tours to the U.S. as spokeswoman for an understanding of the Arab situation. She maintains a hectic schedule of official responsibilities in Jordan, a developing country, where she says her husband encourages women to participate at all levels of society. However, many women still wear the veil. She converted to Islam and adopted an Arabic name, Noor, which means "light." Queen Noor bridges the worlds of Arabic and American culture.

Maharaja of Jaipur

For centuries they were the governing princes of India—maharajas, the great rulers. Their opulent lifestyles were legendary, their eccentricities unrestrained. The princes ruled kingdoms ranging in size from European countries to Disneyland, but a newly independent India stripped them of their sovereignty in 1947. And with that a lavish era of indulgence is said to have vanished.

Today the current Maharaja of Jaipur, known to his friends as "Bubbles," entertains amid a gilded elegance unchanged in generations. His home is a fifteen-hundred-room bejeweled palace where his family has lived for hundreds of years. Dancing girls who were attached to the harem in Bubbles's grandfather's time are still housed in quarters within the palace.

Bubbles was educated in England at Harrow and is a familiar figure on the world's polo circuit. Polo is his favorite indulgence and the greatest source of family pride. Bubbles's father put Jaipur on the polo map when he took 140 ponies to England in 1933 and the team set a winning record that has never been broken. Bubbles spent much of his youth at Rambagh Palace, the family's summer home, which his father turned into one of the world's most exotic hotels. The Jaipur Palace, where the family lives in a private apartment, was turned into a museum. In this way Bubbles's father managed to preserve the lifestyle to which they'd become accustomed. He died in England, playing the game he loved most—polo.

"We are trying to preserve our heritage and culture, as well as the ceremonial traditions," says Bubbles. "We do still have a role to play and the people look up to us as the head of the family, shall we say, to keep these things going, which we do at our own expense." Bubbles is a genial host who welcomed actress Pam Dawber (*pictured at right*) when she taped a "Lifestyles" segment there.

Maharaja of Jaipur (seated far left) with lineup of maharajas.

Above: Prince William amusing members of the British Royal Family at Prince Henry's christening.

152 ᷓ.

Sultan of Brunei

The Sultan of Brunei, believed to be the richest man in the world, rules a tiny South China Sea country with a big bank account. It may be one of the world's smallest monarchies, being no larger than Luxembourg, but it's also one of the world's richest oil-producing nations. With annual oil and gas revenues of $18 billion, the sultanate is like a Middle East sheikdom transplanted to the tropics of Southeast Asia.

The thirty-nine-year-old sultan, Sir Muda Hassanal Bolkiah, belongs to the longest unbroken line of succession of any Asian nation except Japan. His family dynasty has ruled Brunei for the last four hundred years and once even seized Manila and scores of Philippine and Indonesian islands. When Brunei became independent from Britain in 1984, the sultan wanted to throw a little party to celebrate. To make sure there would be enough room for his guests, he had a new palace built. It's just slightly larger than Buckingham Palace and Versailles.

To furnish his 350-acre, 2,300-room palace, he flew in a dozen two-ton chandeliers for the Throne Room and set up dining tables in the Banquet Hall for his 4,000 guests, including Prince Charles and Southeast Asian leaders. The party lasted ten days, with five nights of fireworks that illuminated the palace's twenty-karat-gold dome. Not since the fantasies of *The Arabian Nights* had there been anything quite like it. But the sultan, who has 200 polo ponies, 2 yachts, and 110 cars, including gold- and silver-plated Rolls-Royces, enjoys his sport. And Brunei's foreign reserves could more than handle it, topping $50 billion. So nobody minded the $300-million bill for all this. Or maybe it was $500 million. Who's counting anyway?

The Royal Family of Monaco

. . . .

The tiny Principality of Monaco has basked in splendor as a favorite playground on the European Riviera since the last century. Today old-world society, titled aristocrats, royalty, and dowagers are being eclipsed by the kings of industry, oil-rich Arab sheiks, and American show business stars. They vie for invitations to Europe's most glittering social event, Monaco's annual Red Cross Ball, and crowd the narrow streets for the exciting Grand Prix auto race.

With its historic fairy tale palace and yacht-studded harbor, Monaco attracts millions of visitors, who come to gamble at the casino tables and perhaps catch a glimpse of the royal princesses sporting on the water or in the nightclubs. As the head of the ruling Grimaldi Royal Family, Prince Ranier has spurred new hotel and resort development in his postage-stamp kingdom and

Left: Prince Ranier of Monaco with Princess Stephanie, Princess Caroline and her baby.

enjoys a major share of the multi-million-dollar profits from tourism and casinos.

Since the tragic death of Princess Grace three and a half years ago, the world spotlight has played constantly on her children. Prince Albert, heir to the throne, has had a stint in the French Navy and with a New York law firm and is one of Europe's most dashing young bachelors with a passion for racing boats; Princess Caroline *(pictured right)*, who has captured headlines with her beauty and playboy romances, is married for the second time; and Princess Stephanie *(pictured top)* has blossomed into a striking young woman, much in demand for modeling sessions.

The British Royal Family

The Royal Wedding at Westminster Abbey in July 1981 was a modern fairy tale come true. It transformed twenty-year-old Diana Frances Spencer into the regal Princess of Wales, wife of the future King of England, Prince Charles. Overnight her life shifted from sharing an apartment with three roommates and going out to work as a kindergarten teacher to the glitter and pomp of a palace where she's waited on hand and foot. The girl who raised hamsters and came from an upper-class home that fell apart when her parents divorced won the hearts of everyone in her royal bridal gown with a $4,600 price tag.

Unprepared at first for the responsibilities of the monarchy, she overcame the tensions between personal freedom and public duty and settled into life at Kensington Palace with her dashing polo-playing Prince of Wales, who made no secret of his increasing love and affection for her in public. With her slimmed-down model figure, turquoise-blue eyes, and $300,000-a-year wardrobe, including a $60,000 diamond tiara that once belonged to Queen Mary, the tall blond princess has brought a touch of glamour to the British Royal Family.

She has produced an heir, Prince William, who she insisted accompany her and Prince Charles on an official visit to Australia. Prince Charles bought them a 346-acre, $1-million home, Highgrove House, in Gloucestershire. Princess Diana starts her day with an aerobic workout to a Jane Fonda tape and never begins her official engagements before 10 A.M. The hours between 5 and 7 P.M. are sacrosanct and reserved for bathing and playing with Prince William, who has two nannies. She lunches with Prince Charles at the palace, the most important meal of the day to her, and when they're not entertaining family and friends at home in the evening, the couple love to go out incognito, enjoying the opera and concerts. Princess Diana is particularly close with Queen Elizabeth II, who has reigned for thirty-four years and may step down from the throne for Prince Charles to become King.

Princess Margaret at Mustique estate (above left); Princess Anne (below left); Queen Elizabeth II of England and Prince Philip (right); Prince Charles and Princess Diana (below).

STAYING FIT AND BEAUTIFUL

~-

Debbie Reynolds

Ten years ago Debbie Reynolds found herself flat broke when the accumulated millions from her lifelong career vanished in the shambles of her marriage to shoe store magnate Harry Karl. But Debbie has bounced back with a smash-hit exercise tape, *Do It Debbie's Way,* which went gold and put her back on top of the world again. Her safe, fun, easy workout approach for women "thirty-nine and holding" is a series of routines done to Big Band sounds and it's put her in the forefront of the physical fitness movement. Debbie's showing that age is no barrier and it's never too late to start over.

"I was fifty-one years old. I've been a dancer all my life. I can do two shows a night in Las Vegas," she says. "If I couldn't do Jane Fonda or any of those aero-bic tapes, how could I expect most other women to do them?" Debbie claims even her mother, at seventy-two and with a pacemaker, could do her workout. Debbie is no come-lately to the workout boom. Several years ago she opened her own dance and exercise studio in Hollywood, where stars like Michael Jackson come to rehearse.

Debbie has proved she's a survivor, with one of the most resilient and multifaceted careers in show business. She even opened Debbie's Rentals to recycle all her beautiful furniture, which had been in storage for years. "Life is wonderful; you have to make it wonderful," she says. "You have to just knock down all those barriers and just keep on moving right through it. It's not easy, but we can do it."

Valerie Harper

Exercise turned Valerie Harper's life around, transforming her from homely, rounded Rhoda to the slimmed-down, sleek beauty she is today. All thanks to the coach of the stars Tony Cacciotti, who turned her on to the secret of total fitness. "During the 'Rhoda' years, because I was a chubby character, I really got into some terrible eating habits," she admits. "During those years, I really pigged out and you start hiding in clothes. I used a series of diets. Tony's method changed my entire approach. I realized that thin was not fit. It's almost like I had the wrong goal."

Their training sessions turned into a love affair. Together five years, they have the ultimate buddy system to support each other in their daily workouts. "It doesn't mean you have to become a decathlon champion," says Valerie. "It just means you have to put some physical activity into your life." Tony's approach has already worked for celebrities, including Richard Gere, John Ritter, and Vidal Sassoon. "It's sort of a marriage of mind and body and it's dealing with balance and control," he says. "It's visualizing something mentally before attacking it physically."

Suzy Chaffee

. . . .

She captured the imagination of
millions as a top-ranking Olympian
and world freestyle ski champion
with cover-girl looks. Suzy Chaf-
fee's energy is boundless, as she
pursues a multifaceted career as a
TV personality, model, dancer,
video producer, designer, and fitness book author. She leads a jet-
set lifestyle between homes in New
York and Los Angeles and the playgrounds of the international set.
She's earned handsome salaries as a
corporate spokeswoman, designer of
her own line of skiwear and a
super lightweight ski for women.
She's led health and sports move-
ments, notably as a pioneer of
freestyle skiing, which will become
an Olympic sport in 1988.

Suzy's acrobatic dance move-
ments on skis take everybody's
breath away, but she's gone even
further, performing ballet on roller
skates, ice skates, and water skis.
She's adapting it for skiing and
predicts it will be the next hit of
the Olympics. "My fantasy as a
child was to be a ballerina and
dance down the mountains," she
says. Suzy's done just that, with a
grace and athletic prowess that give
her the edge over everybody—on
snow or sand, land or water.

Greenhouse Spa

When cowgirls from the Lone Star State get the blues, they whittle away those extra pounds at this luxury spa, The Greenhouse, in Dallas. Oil-rich Texas women work it off beside celebrity guests, including Brooke Shields, Cheryl Tiegs, and Liza Minnelli, all willing to pay up to $3,500 a week for the pampering treatment.

The name, Greenhouse, is reflected in this atrium pool area, where each guest is nurtured like a delicate flower. After a rigorous series of stretching, toning, aerobics, and water exercises, you can sink into the whirlpool and steam room to relax or indulge in the gourmet diet meals of 850 calories per day. With all that tender loving body care, the mind and spirit bloom as well.

Vidal Sassoon

Sheer drive and a sharp instinct for trends gave a poor Cockney cutter undreamed-of wealth and power as the head of a hair care and fashion empire that grosses over $100 million a year. Vidal Sassoon is only too aware that he's a living endorsement for his look-good products and, at age fifty-six, he's determined to stay up to his full vigorous potential. With a health and fitness regime that includes swimming, isometrics, workout machines, horse riding, health drinks, a light diet, and fifty vitamin and mineral supplements a day, Sassoon has scaled some ten years off his appearance and he's all set to produce a second family with his new wife, advertising executive Jeanette Hartford. "People say, 'Don't you find it rather stupid at fifty-six, trying to be thirty-five?'" says Sassoon. "I sense we make too much of age."

The son of a carpet salesman from Istanbul who was packed off to an orphanage as a kid, Sassoon has built a fortune since he moved to the U.S. in 1967 and with former wife Beverly became a member of the elite Beverly Hills community. His company has thirty-one salons in six countries, along with stylist schools and expensive sportswear boutiques in London and on exclusive Rodeo Drive.

Ann Turkel

. . . .

Ann Turkel, whose stormy ten-year marriage to Irish actor Richard Harris made as many headlines as her television and film roles, is back in the public eye representing the Unsuit—a sexy bathing suit that lets you tan right through it. It was invented by Hans Buringer, Ann's handsome Viennese-born fiancé and business partner. As the model for the suit, Ann generates booming sales for this business partnership, which keeps the couple shuttling between Ann's luxurious apartment on Manhattan's posh East Side and Hans's hilltop Beverly Hills home.

In California, where show business residents go to any lengths to shape up for the scrutinizing eye of the cameras, Hans hit on another lucrative idea. It's a workout program called Now or Never, which provides Hollywood with the convenience and privacy of a gym-on-wheels. For around $50 an hour, the customized Now or Never truck, loaded with equipment, comes to your home or studio and an instructor gives clients individualized workouts. Ann and Hans's program has been such a hot favorite with celebrities, including Rod and Alana Stewart, Valerie Perrine, Linda Evans, and agent Swifty Lazar, that now they're expanding into franchises and a line of warm-up suits.

Beverly Sassoon

For thirteen years, Beverly Sassoon was married to hair care king Vidal Sassoon before branching out alone in both her private and professional life. Hollywood divorces can cause battles and Beverly had to fight to be allowed to use her famous name for her cosmetics company.

With two top-selling beauty books behind her, Beverly went to work on an exercise book with her daughter Catya, a New York model. She's also a paid lecturer who speaks to women on self-motivation. "Women are finding that more and more we have to go out there and test ourselves and go just a little bit further and try a little bit harder," she says.

Beverly makes sure she takes time out alone, soaking in her luxurious flower-tiled Jacuzzi with stained-glass bay windows. "To me that's more relaxing than a vacation," she says. With her eyes set firmly on the future, marriage is not out of the question. But she's determined never to walk in somebody else's shadow again.

Jack La Lanne

. . . .

At seventy, Jack La Lanne is still the undisputed king of the fitness craze. Today many big-name celebrities have jumped on the multimillion-dollar bandwagon, but Jack was preaching the gospel of getting in shape before they were even born. "I started my first health spa in 1936," he says. "Those were tough days. When you mentioned Jack La Lanne in 1936 in the San Francisco area, people would say: 'That Jack La Lanne, that guy with all those muscles . . . he doesn't eat cakes or pies or ice cream. He's a nut, a crackpot!' "

Today he heads a massive fitness empire, which includes over one hundred health spas coast to coast, training equipment, his own exercise video, books, and dietary supplements. But fitness is as much attitude as biceps and Jack thanks his lucky stars that Elaine, his wife of thirty-one years, has stood by him through it all.

But some of Jack's activities make Elaine's hair stand on end. In a bid to prove that fitness can stop the march of time, Jack has become famous for his outrageous stunts. He swam the icy currents of San Francisco Bay—handcuffed. And on his seventieth birthday—manacled again—he towed seventy boats, loaded with seventy people, for a full mile. "You know, it's easy to die," says Jack. "Dying is easy. It's tough to live. When I think seventy, I don't feel any different now than I have at any point in my life. I believe the sky's the limit."

Donna Mills at Stresa Spa, Lago Maggiore

Among the world-class resorts of international fame is an Italian paradise just an hour's drive northwest of Milan—magical Lago Maggiore. This is where "Knots Landing" star Donna Mills found a tranquil haven at the end of her whirlwind Italian tour. For centuries the rich and famous have found the ultimate escape along the sub-Alpine shores that divide Italy and Switzerland, where lordly villas and deluxe hotels have attracted rulers and aristocrats from Napoleon to Vanderbilt. It was here, at the palatial Grand Hôtel des Iles Borromées, that Grand Duchess Alexandra of Russia carved her name in a windowpane with her diamond ring . . . and it was here that Ernest Hemingway's hero in *A Farewell to Arms* convalesced.

The tiny town of Stresa was Donna's pick from among the many fishing villages that surround Lago Maggiore. Donna came to the hotel to escape the rigors of Hollywood. Inside this sumptuous palace lies the secret of the rich and famous—an Italian fountain of youth, the Stresa Spa. "The spa is wonderful," she says. "It's totally designed to make you feel pampered. They cover your body with a mixture of natural substances and herbs and put you in hydrotherapy. It was very calming." Nothing beats this soothing spa for getting rid of Stresa!

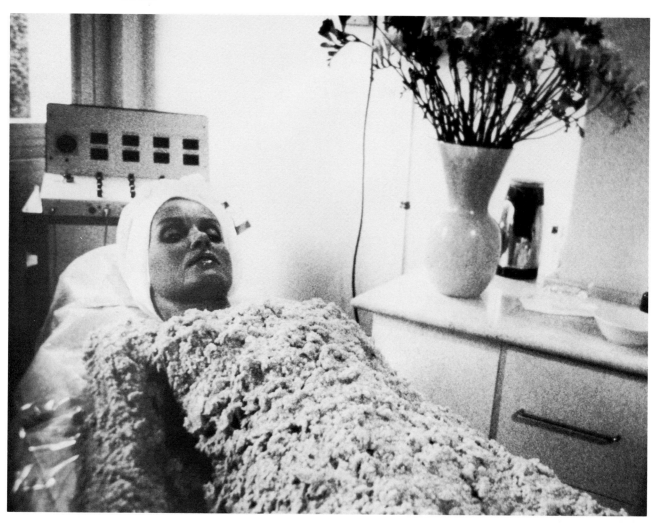

Mary Kay Ash

Mary Kay Ash has turned a formula for cleansing cream into a formula for success and inspired millions of women to look and feel their best. Twenty years after the appearance of her first product, Mary Kay Cosmetics has annual sales in excess of $300 million and boasts of having more women who earn over $50,000 a year than any company in America.

Her sales force of two hundred thousand women is spurred on by her unique personal recognition—the company's annual seminar in Dallas, where she gives away $15 million in prizes, including diamonds, gorgeous furs, and big pink Cadillacs. Despite the riches

Mary Kay's beauty empire has brought her, she prefers to remain living in a tranquil Dallas setting, where her circular-shaped home—symbolizing love—is decorated in her favorite color: pink.

Behind Mary Kay's success lies her ability to whip up company spirit and an infectious enthusiasm for selling beauty that pays off in huge profits for everyone. "The thing of which I'm most proud is having gotten so many women to understand that they really are terrific and they can do anything in this world that they want to," she says.

That sense of confidence has turned a $5,000 investment into one of the largest cosmetics empires in the world.

Adrien Arpel

Her face is her business and the business is beauty. One out of every five American women powder their noses with her product. Hers is a cosmetics empire worth over $18 million a year and hers is the face that launched it. She's Adrien Arpel. "I started at seventeen years of age with $400 in baby-sitting money," she says. "And it really is the original Cinderella story; it's the only-in-America story. That really does happen."

At nineteen Adrien had seventy-six salon franchises and banked her first million. "It grew like top seed because there was a real need for what we were saying: 'Look like yourself, but better!' " In clinics from Hong Kong to Chile, women are transforming themselves with the famous Adrien Arpel makeover.

Adrien has been married to real estate investor Ron Newman for twenty-four years and they have a beautiful daughter, Lauren. They divide their time between their fabulous New York East Side triplex penthouse overlooking the river and their Southampton $4-million beach house.

SPORTING

Kentucky Derby

In the dramatic and high-risk world of horse racing, there are the gamblers, the high rollers, and those true connoisseurs for whom racing is a high-stakes business.

Horse breeding has been called the most elegant form of crap shooting in the world and it's no surprise that where there's gold, the rich and famous are there, too. Every year cash-laden Europeans, Arab sheiks, and a star or two come to the exclusive Kentucky Yearling Sales in search of a Derby winner.

The Kentucky Derby is America's answer to the elegant English Ascot. There are the fabulous hats, the tailgate affairs with the official mint julips, the private boxes worth over $6,000, and of course the stars, including John Forsythe, Larry Hagman, Priscilla Presley, Olivia Newton-John, Diane Sawyer, and Gene Hackman, who join the horsey set for a week of parties and dinner dances. The Kentucky Derby is the ultimate horse race, with over $18 million wagered in 1984, the year Swale raced and won under the famous silks of Clairborne Farm. Swale was worth over $50 million at his untimely death. In 1985 the laurels went to winner Spend a Buck (pictured), ridden by jockey Angel Cordero, Jr.

Polo

Polo, the sport of kings and maharajas, demands a well-heeled—and -hooved—following. Prince Charles's passion for polo costs him around $108,000 a year—ten times Britain's average wage. Today it costs $9,500 a year to keep a polo pony and good players maintain a string of ten! And that price doesn't include the cost of polo sticks, tackle, saddles, transport, and running costs. Britain's elite corps of polo players fork out a total of $40.5 million a year to indulge in their favorite sport.

Polo has become the hottest game in town for Hollywood celebrities, who have attracted a whole new entourage of fans to the excitement of pounding hooves and cracking mallets. Among the polo set are stars David Hasselhoff, Larry Hagman, Cliff Robertson, Robert Wagner, and Stefanie Powers, carrying on the tradition that began with Will Rogers, who took the game out to the American West.

Left: Prince Charles. Below (left to right): Stefanie Powers, Pamela Sue Martin, Stacey Keach, William Devane, and Robert Wagner at polo fund-raiser.

Jan Stephenson

. . . .

She's been dubbed "The Marilyn
Monroe of Pro Golf" and she's
turned it into an all-star, money-
making machine that earns her
more dollars off the course than
on. Her seductive pose for a golf
magazine in 1981 caused a storm
that split pro ranks and a poster
showing her in Marilyn Monroe's
famous skirt-blown pose contrib-
uted to her commercial sex appeal.

But the thirty-four-year-old, blue-
eyed, blond Jan Stephenson is
much more than just another pretty
face. She's earned fifteen pro titles,
including the tournament she had
dreamed of winning ever since she
was a twelve-year-old in her native
Australia—the U.S. Open. Jan's
tournament prize money totals
nearly $1 million and she pulls in
four times that much from endorsements. Her business projects
include a revolutionary line of golf
shoes and an exercise video.

Jan, who's married to Texas
oilman Eddie Vossler, has homes in
Phoenix and Fort Worth. But between golf tournaments and her
business, she spends so much time
on the road that she got her own
Citation jet—and learned how to
fly it. It's one way she found to
grab time with her husband—mid-
air between her hectic engage-
ments. "It's a chance for the two of
us to be up there together, which is
kind of fun," says Jan. "Just the two
of us at 37,000 feet and that really
is a neat feeling."

Dorothy Hamill

. . . .

At age twenty she was America's sweetheart on ice—the shy and giggly girl from Greenwich, Connecticut, who glided away with an Olympic gold medal at Innsbruck, Austria. Her triumphs on ice were mirrored by her fairy-tale Hollywood wedding to Dean Martin, Jr., in 1982. She earns millions from product endorsements and contracts, which have brought her a beautiful home in Los Angeles and another in Connecticut, where she can be close to her parents.

The long years of training and discipline paid off with undreamed-of success for the girl who started skating at eight years old in hand-me-down clothes on a pond behind her grandparents' house. But behind the shining, smiling public image is a dark secret. Dorothy's mother, who was by her side during the early struggles on the road, had a long battle with cancer. That pain and the trauma of her divorce after only two years of marriage have brought profound changes for Dorothy. "I've learned a lot about myself and what I value. I've been without a lot, not making any money at times, and there were times when my mom didn't know where she was going to get the next meal to put on the training table. Now I know that money doesn't make you happy. People and family are the things that count. I'm glad I've learned that."

Gambling

In the high-rolling world of gambling, no expense is spared to woo the big spenders, who get their sport courting Lady Luck at extravagant palaces designed to pamper every whim. The most spectacular of all is the new ultramodern Trump's Castle. The Sands Hotel in Atlantic City offers exclusive accommodations at the Plaza Club, reserved for special clients who don't flinch at staking at least a quarter of a million dollars' play money for a night's fun. The members-only club offers seven distinctively different suites with lavish amenities and ocean views, butlers, intimate dining, and a huge Jacuzzi to soak up the joys of winning a fortune at the tables.

In Las Vegas, gamblers are enticed with glamorous shows and glittering hotels, like the spectacular $15-million, eighteen-story Golden Nugget. But you can't always judge a checkbook by its cover and downtown there's a little hotel with a big bankroll at Binion's Horseshoe—and they'll take any size bet. High-stakes gambling is big business at Binion's, where they've seen over a million dollars on the table at once and every pot runs around $50,000. Some gamblers have been known to lose and win $800,000 in one night. But they always come back with that dream of a winning streak that will break the bank.

Plaza Club suite at Sands Hotel, Atlantic City. Inset: Binion's, Las Vegas.

"LIFESTYLES SALUTE TO THE WORLD'S BEST"

In the highly popular "Lifestyles Salute to the World's Best" TV special, a galaxy of superstars jetted off for a glittering journey to the world's number one hot spots —the very best of everything . . . everywhere. Our "Lifestyles" cameras traveled over a million miles to bring you an armchair view of the ultimate traveling experience. Here is a sampling of that count-down. . . .

World's Best Cruise Ship

The Royal Princess

From the lavish two-acre decks of *The Royal Princess,* Connie Stevens and I hosted the "Lifestyles Salute to the World's Best" TV special. The newest, most glamorous and luxurious cruise ship ever built marks the renaissance of romance on the high seas—it's dubbed "The Super Love Boat."

All of the ship's six hundred staterooms are outside, with picture windows looking onto the ocean. Original artworks adorn the soft-toned decor of this floating palace, where every passenger is treated like royalty, with amenities that include sumptuous dining, a spa, gym, and two whirlpools. For the ultimate in seagoing splendor, the Princess and Royal suites have their own private verandas, hot tubs, and king-sized beds. The cost of this deluxe accommodation on an eleven-night Panama Canal and Caribbean Island cruise: $7,300.

Inset: Lana Turner and Stewart Granger filming an episode for "The Love Boat."

Grandest Hotels

1. The Oriental, Bangkok
2. Shangri-la, Singapore
3. Imperial, Tokyo
4. Mandarin, Hong Kong
5. Connaught, London
6. Ritz, Paris
7. Vier Jahreszeiten, Hamburg
8. Baur au Lac, Zurich
9. Ritz, Madrid
10. Plaza-Athénée, Paris

Resort Hotels

1. Hôtel du Cap, French Riviera
2. Kapalua Bay, Maui
3. Hôtel de Paris, Monte Carlo
4. Las Brisas, Acapulco
5. La Samanna, St. Martin
6. Marbella Club, Spain
7. The Breakers, Palm Beach, Florida
8. Mauna Lani, Hawaii
9. The Palace Hotel, Gstaad
10. Little Dix Bay, British Virgin Islands

Romantic Hotels

1. The Hassler, Rome
2. The Carlyle, New York
3. The Mansion, Dallas
4. La Mamounia, Marrakech
5. Mayfair Regent, New York
6. Bel Air Hotel, Bel Air, California
7. L'Ermitage, Beverly Hills
8. Baumanière, Les Baux, France
9. L'Hôtel, Paris
10. Blakes, London

Gourmet Dining

1. Boyer les Crayères, Reims, France
2. Giradet, Switzerland (near Lucerne)
3. Paul Bocuse, Lyons, France
4. Taillevent, Paris
5. Connaught Grill, London
6. Latour, Singapore
7. Fontainebleau, Tokyo
8. Le Moulin de Mougins, Cannes
9. L'Orangerie, Los Angeles
10. Lutece, New York

Most Romantic Restaurants

1. Michel's, Hawaii
2. Waterside Inn, England
3. Baumanière, Les Baux, France
4. English House, London
5. Colombe d'Or, St.-Paul-de-Vence, France
6. Le Restaurant, Los Angeles
7. Bistro Garden, Beverly Hills
8. La Mer, Honolulu
9. Ernie's, San Francisco

Hotel du Cap

PHOTO CREDITS